CURIOSITIES SERIES

Maine Curiosities

QUIRKY CHARACTERS, ROADSIDE ODDITIES & OTHER OFFBEAT STUFF

TIM SAMPLE
AND
STEVE BITHER

SECOND EDITION

INSIDERS' GUIDE®
GUILFORD, CONNECTICUT
AN IMPRINT OF THE GLOBE PEQUOT PRESS

The prices and rates in this guidebook were confirmed at press time. We recommend, however, that you call establishments before traveling to obtain current information.

INSIDERS' GUIDE®

Text design by Nancy Freeborn

All photos by the authors except the following: Page 7: courtesy Jane Burke, photo © Rich Entel; p. 21: courtesy Colonial Theater photo © Michael Hurley; p. 23: courtesy Bennett's Gem and Jewelry; p. 44: courtesy Farnsworth Art Museum, photo by Maureen (Leonard) Campbell; p. 55: courtesy WERU Radio Station; p. 65: courtesy Bill and Kathleen Hallinan; p.68: courtesy L.L. Bean; p. 103: © Michael A. Clark; p. 123: courtesy Maine Scene Inc., photo © Lyman Owen; p. 131: courtesy Graylock Productions, photo © Will Cook; p. 156: University of Maine Special Collections Folger Library; p. 163: courtesy Crown of Maine Hot Air Balloon Festival, photo © Milt Smith, Presque Isle; p. 167: © Jere DeWaters; p. 176: courtesy Shakers Sabbathday Lake Community; pp. 181, 182: courtesy Red Arrow Snowmobile Club, photos by Dana Deprey; p. 203: courtesy Roger Snow; p. 212: courtesy Eliot Winslow; p. 218: courtesy Maine Scene Inc.; p. 219: courtesy Maine Scene Inc., photo © Lyman Owen; p. 230: courtesy Joe Perham; p. 241: photo © Jere DeWaters; p. 249: photo © DeLorme; p. 256: photo of Tim Sample © Kevin Sample-Wilcox; photo of Steve Bither © Ted Haider.

ISBN-13: 978-0-7627-4029-1
ISBN-10: 0-7627-4029-9

Manufactured in the United States of America
Second Edition/First Printing

Kayce? Sorry, I don't know anyone by that name.
For Kevin! my marvelous wife, with love and respect.

—Tim Sample

With love for Paula, my favorite cowgirl.

—Steve Bither

Contents

So You Think You Know MAINE?

This book has been easy and difficult to write and rewrite. It's easy because "Curiosities and Oddities" are the rule, rather than the exception, in the state of Maine. We're all quirky characters, and every road in every town has some sort of roadside oddity.

It's difficult because there is a cottage industry in Maine that calls attention to how we, as a state and as a people, are unique and different from the rest of the world. We have to show how OUR collection of quirky stuff is unique and different from the stuff displayed by the guys in the other cottages.

Tim is the natural choice for writing the definitive book of Maine curiosities. He's driven everywhere in the state, talking and listening to fellow Mainers and generally noticing and commenting on the state of the state in his work as a Down East humorist, writer, illustrator, and correspondent for *CBS Sunday Morning*. Steve has been an observer of Maine life, both as a singer/songwriter/keyboard player with the Wicked Good Band and as a lawyer for Maine people. Way back in the1970s, we played together in a couple of bands, including the Dubious Brothers, where we began developing humor skits and generally trying to entertain each other, in the face of sparse, drunk, and inattentive audiences.

In 2001 Tim started writing the first edition of this book. He got a little stuck in the middle of the process—that's what happens when you think too much about what you are doing. Anyway, he called Steve, and together the two of us put together a nondefinitive list of things that would qualify as "Quirky Characters, Roadside Oddities & Other Offbeat Stuff." The fun was in the discovery—meeting new people and seeing how proud they were of the things they had done or the stuff they had. The book was on the local best-seller list for several months, and it made us some new friends. It also generated the usual responses from people who tell us about even more odd stuff that we have to comment on or see.

The editors at Globe Pequot asked us to prepare a second edition in August 2005. After we spent time trying to identify new oddities and modifying our reports about existing ones, we got to work, riding the bumpy back roads, jamming the phone lines, and surfing the Net for quirky Maine stuff. About a third of this book is new material, and it was as much fun to discover as it was the first time around. As Tim said in the introduction to the first *Maine Curiosities:* Getting there isn't the point of the journey. It's what you see along the way that makes the journey memorable.

This book isn't exactly a tourist guide. A lot of things listed as curiosities or oddities aren't there any more—except as memories of things that have left a footprint on our collective spirit. You will also see some of the offbeat ways we do things, like deorganizing towns or bowling candlepins. But even this book is not the final word on the subject. We hope that our collection of Maine oddities will whet your appetite for more of the same. This is just the tip of the iceberg, folks. As long as there are long, cold winters followed by tourist-jammed summers, you can bet that Mainers will continue to create newer, better, and more outlandish roadside attractions. Why do we do it? Who knows? Maybe it's just to get you to stop and ask directions to the next roadside attraction. Ayuh. That's probably it. We always get a kick out of it when you ask directions.

The Telstar Bubble

Andover

The little town of Andover wasn't even on the map until the bubble came. "You'd see Byron and Rumford, but the town of Andover was so small they wouldn't even put it on most maps," said Roger, a guy I happened to meet who grew up in Andover in the 1950s and 1960s. Back then the town was so small that Roger's graduating class of seventeen was the largest in Andover High School history. Everything changed when Andover became the site, in the early 1960s, of TXX1, a tracking antenna for one of the earliest communications satellites, Telstar. America was just entering the space age in those days. The Tornados' song, "Telstar," with its space-age organ and guitar sounds, was the rage. And, with the making of a space bubble, Andover was put on the map.

The engineers at Bell Labs developed the antenna-satellite system, along with government-funded Project Relay, using parts from the Nike, Zeus, and Hercules rocket systems. (No, they didn't have "swooshes" on them.) The engineers needed a location free from the interference of microwave and other transmissions. Andover sat in a natural bowl, and it was thought that the microwaves wouldn't interfere with the operation of the station. A sensitive antenna, or horn, was constructed for the transmission of telephone, television, and data communications between outer space and Andover. The most interesting part of the scheme was "the bubble": Built of treated canvas, the giant bubble was designed to keep the elements of weather off the antenna.

The bubble brought opportunities for local involvement. Local workers made top dollar clearing the land for the bubble. At first, the public was invited inside the bubble to gawk at the antenna, but the constant traffic had an impact on the atmospheric pressure inside. So the "bubbleites" (as they were called) built a viewing area, a "fishbowl," to observe the antenna horn as it circled on its track following an invisible star. Some folks in town were less than excited about the bubble; they thought the project was a waste of government money. Other folks were certain the government was doing something it wasn't telling us about, and that UFOs were being tracked. Some folks, whether they were local or not, took potshots at the bubble with their hunting rifles (at least, they said, they couldn't miss hitting it). David Belanger, who worked at the bubble, said a crew once counted seven bullet holes in the skin of the bubble.

In its heyday, the station employed about ninety people, many of them professionals from New York and other foreign lands. These people built nice homes and brought some money into town. Naturally, they also brought with them their own views of how things should be run locally, which caused some resentment.

By the 1980s the bubble had outlasted its usefulness. Newer forms of satellite dishes withstood the elements better. According to David, it cost $100,000 to heat the bubble, which made it economically unfeasible. In 1985 the bubble was decommissioned. Then it was dismantled. "Al Bancroft, a local resident, tore it down and took the scrap metal to the junkyard," says David. Local people took discarded lights and doorknobs from the site, and some folks actually took chunks of the bubble as souvenirs of the early space age. So, if you're looking for the bubble, you'll find it in pieces in local barns. The cutting-edge technology that got the station going was replaced by fiber optics. Now owned by WorldCom, the antenna traffic is focused on transmitting to countries whose infrastructures are not as up-to-date as ours. The antenna station, no longer in a bubble, employs about seven people.

Duke's Barber "Pole": As Maine Goes, So Goes the Nation

Augusta

Of course, it's always easy to be a Monday-morning quarterback on these things. Still, I feel pretty confident in saying that if Dan Rather and the rest of the network TV news anchors had taken the time to put their high-priced consultants on hold for five minutes and make a call to Augusta, Maine, on Election Night 2000, they all might have ended up with a lot less egg on their collective faces.

Like it or not, exit polls and other forms of modern-day prognostication have become an integral part of election news coverage. Taking the public pulse in this manner is a multibillion-dollar business. But, as the flip-flopping predictions of newscasters in the Y2K presidential elections pointed out, sometimes even the most scientific poll results that money can buy are embarrassingly off the mark.

Which brings us to Duke Dulac, who, for nearly half a century, has been "lowering ears" at Duke's Barber Shop, which is located alongside the traffic rotary on the west side of the Kennebec River in Augusta. You want accuracy in your political polls? You got it at Duke's. For the past thirty-three years, besides cutting hair (three chairs, no waiting), Duke has been polling his customers and using their ballots to predict the outcome of upcoming elections. How's his track record so far? Actually, it's perfect, thank you very much. That's right, when it comes to calling the winner of the race for the White House, Duke's "barber pole" has a 100 percent rate of accuracy. Not impressed? Since instituting his decidedly unscientific survey back in 1973, he's also had a 100 percent success rate in predicting the outcome of Maine's gubernatorial races. If you factor in races for the Senate and House of Representatives, local and statewide offices, and the inevitable referendum issues that are so popular here in the Pine Tree State, his poll still boasts an astounding 97 percent success rate.

A case in point: According to Duke, "When Cohen [senator and later secretary of defense William Cohen of Bangor] ran against Libby Mitchell in '84, he came in and I gave him a printout of how he was gonna do. Out of 350 people, we had him getting 87 percent of the vote and Libby 13 percent. It came out he ended up getting 86 percent and Libby 14 percent. He sent me a letter a couple days after the election that said, 'Nice job, Duke. Try harder next time. You were off one

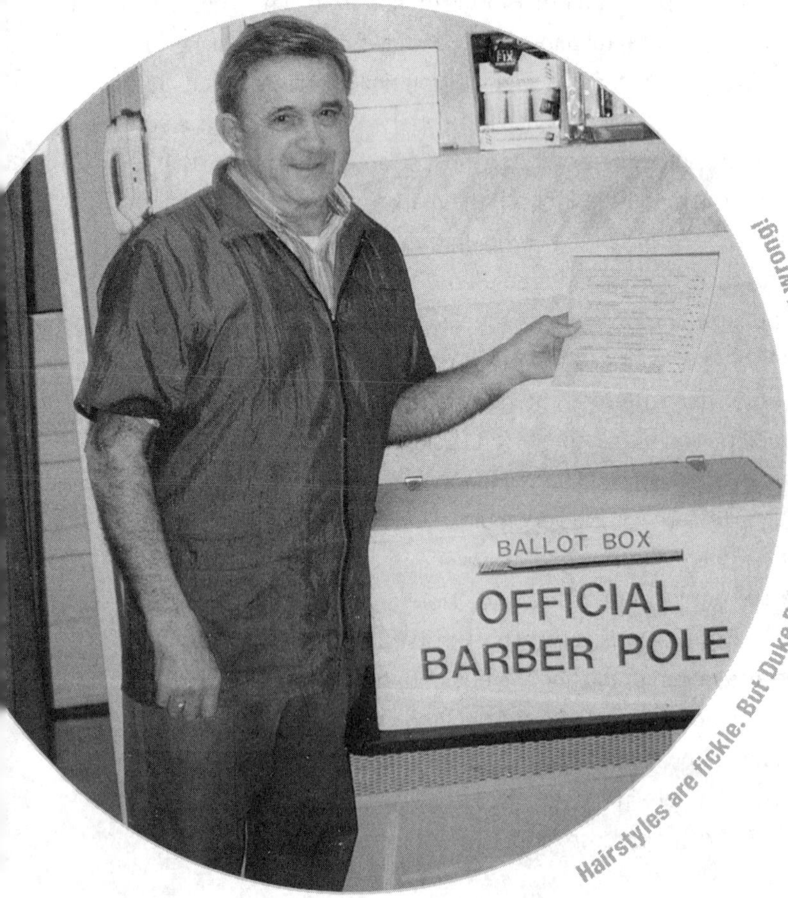

Hairstyles are fickle. But Duke Dulac's "Barber Pole" is never wrong!

point.' So I said to him when I saw him at Jock's [former Maine governor John "Jock" McKernan] inauguration, we were off one point because you went home and took a nap after I showed you how well you were doing!"

What's he doing that all the big shots aren't? Well, according to Duke, it's just common sense. He believes that when people are contacted by telephone pollsters, they know that somehow these folks got hold of their phone number, and, despite assurances of anonymity, their responses tend to be influenced by what they think the caller wants to hear. According to Duke, the same is true with exit polls. For instance, in the weeks prior to a statewide vote on a gay rights referendum in Maine ("A touchy one," says Duke), virtually all the polls showed the bill passing by a comfortable margin. Duke's customers accurately predicted its defeat. Duke figures that since people didn't want to be branded homophobes, they said whatever they thought a questioner wanted to hear. But in the privacy of the voting booth they voted the way they really thought. The results may not have been the best reflection on Mainers' social attitudes, but they sure were accurate.

How private is the barber poll? Voting at Duke's is virtually identical to the real thing. He uses real ballots obtained from the city, the same ones people will see when they step into the booth. ("Sometimes they'll stamp 'sample' on 'em," he says.) And the process is completely anonymous. Instead of perusing a three-month-old copy of *Field and Stream* or *Sports Illustrated,* customers perched on the chrome-and-vinyl chairs lining the south wall simply mark their ballots, fold them in half, and drop them in the official ballot box. No one sticks a camera in their face and asks them how they voted. Nobody knows their phone number or mailing address. No salesman will call.

Duke figures that his clientele is a pretty representative cross section of average Maine folks. Consequently, when the ballots are counted at the end of the day, Duke knows what the people of Maine are thinking.

Let's just say it's awfully hard to argue with his track record. By the way, Duke didn't spend any time agonizing along with the rest of us over the unprecedented Bush/Gore presidential election cliffhanger: He knew who the winner would be at least three weeks before election night. When it comes to picking the next president, Duke has never, *ever,* been wrong.

Jane Burke Loves Maine (and Vice Versa)

Augusta

Jane Burke describes her tiny, campy, turquoise-and-white, kitsch-laden 1957 Vagabond house trailer as "a silver bullet lodged in the throat of state government." That statement refers to the fact that Jane's trailer, a virtual shrine to her fabulous, trademark off-the-wall visual style, is tucked away on a secluded lot, just a stone's throw from the capitol in Augusta. Not that Jane is throwing any stones, ever. She's a lot more likely to pick 'em up, paint 'em Day-Glo orange, and line her driveway with 'em.

No pop star from A(retha) to Z(appa) ever had a better time playing in the fields of popular "kulchah" than Jane Burke. Jane's whole raison d'être since she arrived on this planet seems to have been inventing, reinventing, and re-reinventing herself and reinterpreting the world around her. She claims to do this mostly for her own amusement. But it also serves as great entertainment for those lucky passersby who stray into her highly charged, brilliantly hued force field.

According to Jane, her adolescence was characterized by a "need for notoriety." It's hard to argue that point with a woman who walks around with half of her hair dyed a brassy blond and the other half a generic brown. Of her hairstyle, Jane simply states, "I had to entertain myself." Early in her career, in the absence of any volunteers, Jane started her own Jane Burke Fan Club, complete with regular newsletters describing her day-to-day activities—applying makeup, raking blueberries, that sort of thing.

You can laugh all you want (believe me, Jane would approve), but eventually some pretty high-profile people ended up on the Jane Burke bandwagon. A few summers back actress Kirstie Alley became a fan. "I painted a lot of furniture for her home here in Maine," says Jane. "And I painted murals for the children." After thoroughly Jane Burke–izing her place in Maine, Alley persuaded Jane to leave the state of Maine (not an easy thing to do), and our heroine spent several months painting furniture, murals, and other stuff in the star's California home.

Impersonating a Maine lawn ornament is but one of Jane Burke's many talents.

After finishing up out west, she headed to New York to collaborate with some other decorative painters on the former apartment of the late legendary screen idol Greta Garbo. But as outrageously attention-grabbing as Jane can be, at heart she's a "serious" artist with zero interest in coasting along with the "artist to the stars" bit. "I'm really uncomfortable with that whole thing," says Jane. "In L.A. so many people seemed to be, like, in awe about all celebrities. It really bothered me." It also bothered her that folks took her art more seriously just because she had worked for a "big-name star."

Whatever Jane has done with her creativity, it's the opposite of selling out. For her, creativity is a calling, almost like a religion, and she has little patience with those who view art as an afterthought. According to Jane, "If you put the beauty, the creativity, THE ART first, then the other things will eventually . . ."

She pauses. "Well," she says, "you're not gonna starve."

But you might come close. Jane talked to me matter-of-factly about the time she had to choose between buying food and purchasing a cassette of new music she wanted to listen to. She chose to feed her soul. Clearly, she made the right choice.

These days Jane no longer lives in her famous Maine trailer (featured prominently in a recent documentary by filmmaker David Brooks). According to Jane, "I'm using it sometimes as a handbag, sometimes as a mini-office, and sometimes as a home for unwed fathers." She hasn't slowed down much, though. In addition to graphic art projects and performing with her band, Jane Loves Maine, she's added stand-up comedy to her stage act and eagerly anticipates celebrating the year 2007 as "The Year of the Eyebrow."

Eyebrow? "Oh yes," says Jane matter-of-factly. "My serpentine eyebrow [that's the hand-painted extension of her natural brow that swirls dramatically across half her face] and I are celebrating fifteen years together." My goodness. Has it been fifteen years already? "Well," Jane admits, "it isn't actually fifteen years, but that sounds better than thirteen or fourteen." Ah yes, of course! Perhaps that statement in itself best captures the elusive, eclectic, mercurial Maine essence of Jane Burke. Whatever sounds better, looks better, makes you smile, laugh, or think twice about the things you see every day, that's what Jane Burke is all about. As far as I can tell, Jane loves Maine, and the feeling is mutual.

BORDER TRIVIA

Maine is basically diamond-shaped, with four major sides. As we learned in school, it is the only state in the continental United States that has only one other state bordering it. (Maine is also the only state with one syllable—you could look that up.)

According to the Maine Department of Transportation and the International Boundary Commission, Maine's borders look like this:

Border with New Hampshire: 140 miles (but it costs you a buck to get there)

Border with Quebec, Canada: 292 miles

Border with New Brunswick, Canada: 319 miles

Maine coastline (nooks and crannies): 3,460 miles

Elvis Comes to Maine

Augusta

The brass plaque in the lobby of the Augusta Civic Center commemorates the evening of May 24, 1977. That date marks the only Maine appearance of "The King," rock 'n' roll pioneer Elvis Presley. The legendary zeal of Elvis's fans being what it is, I just assumed that the dull, worn spots on the left side of the plaque were the result of thousands of true believers lovingly caressing its polished surface. Dave Jowdry, who manages the facility, acknowledges that that's what a lot of folks think. It makes a great story, he says. But the truth is a bit more pedestrian.

The shrine was apparently defaced when some overly enthusiastic Republicans (obviously not Presley fans) hastily taped a campaign sign to its surface during a convention a few years back. Not to worry, says Dave (who attended the Elvis show and, although he never met the man, is proud to say that he glimpsed the back of The King's head backstage surrounded by a phalanx of the Memphis Mafia). The Maine Elvis fan club is planning to raise funds for a shiny new replacement.

Brief though his sojourn in Maine was, Elvis left some lasting impressions. After the show in Augusta, he spent the night at the Sheraton Tara in South Portland. According to longtime Sheraton employee Mavis Spaltro, Elvis and his entourage took over the entire eighth and ninth floors of the East Tower. The King himself was ensconced in Room 807. No employees were allowed on the floor with Elvis during his stay. Nevertheless, several managed to glimpse—you guessed it—the back of his head. That famous head presumably spent at least some time on the bathroom floor, since when he left, the management found Elvis's autograph on the underside of the sink. By the way, if you're a hardcore fan, you can still book Room 807. But the sink is gone, torn out and auctioned off as a souvenir during renovations several years back.

Like his legendary life, the Elvis in Maine story ends on a blue note. Elvis was booked at the same hotel for his second Maine appearance on August 16, 1977, the very day he was found dead in his home at Graceland.

Is Paul Bunyan Really a Mainer?

Bangor

My best friend hails from Minnesota, so it was only natural that she was a bit skeptical when I took her to visit Bangor's famous Paul Bunyan statue and tried to convince her that the legendary giant lumberjack got his start here in the Pine Tree State. I suppose you'd get the same reaction from most Minnesotans. By all accounts, Minnesota is practically littered with Paul Bunyan statues, including an 18-footer in the town of Brainard, which was erected more than twenty years before our "Paul" and features the big guy's famous sidekick, Babe the blue ox. On the other hand, if we're talkin' big guys, Paul in Bangor would have the edge. At 31 feet, our Paul stands head and shoulders above his western rival. And if our woodsman is missing his ox, at least he's got a peavey.

What's a peavey? Well, it seems that back in 1858 a blacksmith from Stillwater, Maine (remember the name of the town, OK?), was watching the local log drivers on the Stillwater River as they separated the jammed-up logs with crude pikes. Struck by inspiration, he retired to his shop and started to hammer out his new invention. A few days later he emerged with the first peavey, a sharp iron pike attached to a long wooden handle with a hook, or "dog," hanging from the underside. The peavey was a brilliantly simple tool. The leverage provided by the pike, iron hook, and long wooden handle made the dangerous task of rolling logs on the swift river easier, faster, and much safer. It was an immediate hit, and almost a century and a half later the Snow and Neally Company is still making peaveys and selling them around the globe.

So what about Stillwater? My friend grew up next door to the town of Stillwater, Minnesota, which was founded by lumbermen who had migrated west from guess where? Ayuh . . . Stillwater, Maine. I figure those folks just brought the Paul Bunyan story to Minnesota along with 'em.

It's the big guy, Paul Bunyan, holding the world's biggest peavey.

UNCLE HENRY'S SWAP 'N' SELL: A LITERARY BARGAIN

Have you priced a paperback novel lately? Let's just say they've come a long way from the days of the "dime novel." If the thought of parting with nearly a ten spot for the privilege of toting the latest best-seller to the beach makes you blanch, help is on the way.

Every Thursday, for only a buck seventy-five, at just about any store in Maine with a cash register, you can pick up the latest copy of *Uncle Henry's Weekly Swap or Sell It Guide.* What you'll get at this bargain basement price is nearly 400 pages of tiny print at a fraction of what you'd pay for the same thing from John Grisham or Stephen King.

It's not the same you say? Those folks are great storytellers? Well, I maintain there's plenty of great writing and storytelling in Uncle Henry's . . . you just have to use your imagination a bit. You see, those famous best-selling authors get paid millions for their stuff, so they can afford to sit around on their yachts, sipping champagne and spinning long complicated tales full of romance and drama, crime and punishment. But the writers you'll be reading each week in Uncle Henry's are just workin' stiffs like you and me. They can't sit around waiting for the muse to stroll in the door—they only get a half hour for lunch! Besides, the free ad form only allows you thirty words (including the town and the phone number) so Uncle Henry's writers have a built-in incentive for avoiding verbosity and complex plot lines; they just cut right to the chase. Here's just one example (and there are plenty more in each action-packed issue):

"Will swap, slightly used, size 18 wedding dress, would like to trade for 357 Magnum!"

That's only fifteen words, but I think you'll agree there's a whole novel in there between the lines.

Belt Sander Races

Bath

I'm sure that plenty of grand schemes have been hatched over a couple of cold brews at the now defunct/always funky Triple R Bar in Bath, but it's unlikely that many of them ever developed beyond the stage of pool table banter at the legendary biker bar. The exception that proves the rule is the Belt Sander Races, which have been held regularly for the past two decades or so on the first Sunday in March at the Bath Elks Lodge. The event is run by the United Bikers of Maine, and all proceeds are donated to the Maine Children's Cancer Program.

If you're not familiar with belt sander racing, don't feel too bad. According to Mac McCreary of Woolwich, the sport is still in its infancy. The turnout for these races doesn't rival NASCAR crowds (although, come to think of it, the per capita beer consumption just might). On a good year you're apt to find two- or three-dozen competitors each with a half dozen or so loyal "fans" egging 'em on.

McCreary's obviously a big fan of belt sander racing. He says that the inspiration for the event came in the early to mid-1980s. A bunch of local carpenters had stopped by the Triple R for a few beers on the way home from work. Some alchemy involving professional pride, alcohol, and testosterone took place, and a new sport was born. Makes sense

Mainers clearly invest more in their belt sanders than in their advertising budgets.

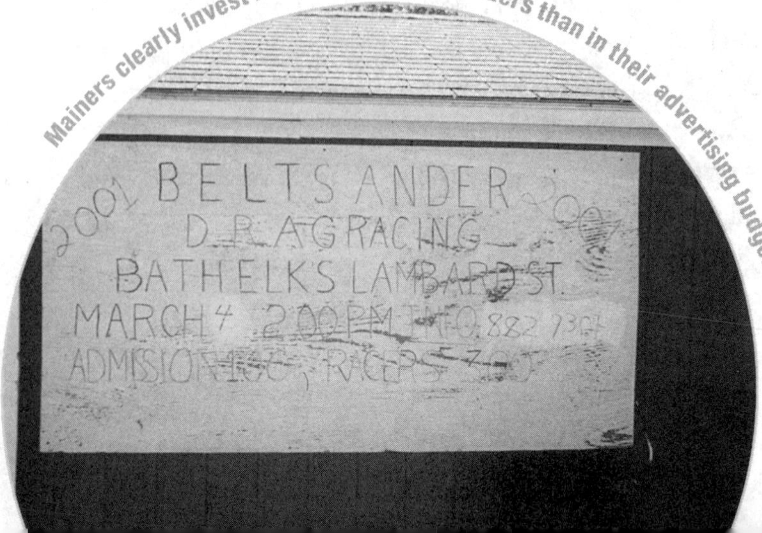

to me. I believe that, over the years, these same conditions have contributed to the creation of many innovative recreational pursuits, everything from mud wrestling to cockroach racing.

Belt sander racers compete in either stock or modified classes on two parallel plywood tracks about 40 feet long. Rails on the sides keep these hopped-up hand tools from veering off course, and there's a thick foam rubber pad to cushion the impact at the end of the race. A lot of the contestants just use their tools from work. But in the modified class it's a different story. Hot rod secrets of winning belt sander racers include adding weights to the front end for traction and removing the trigger and hard-wiring the electrics for a faster start. Of course, a flashy paint job with a couple of sponsors' logos certainly doesn't hurt.

McCreary says the racers don't really have a sophisticated timing system or anything. Whichever sander smashes into the foam pad first wins. But, he estimates that a fast tool in the stock class would run the track in one and a half to two seconds, whereas a heavily modified unit might easily shave a half second off that time.

As I talked to McCreary, the date of the annual event kept bouncing around in my skull: The first Sunday in March. The first Sunday in March. Then it dawned on me. The reason why this exciting new sport would just naturally have to have been created here in Maine is it's a reeeealllly long winter and there just ain't a lot goin' on.

Loony Lagoon

Bath

According to Philip Day, the septuagenarian sculptor, painter, and creator of the Loony Lagoon in Bath, the inspiration for his roadside work-in-progress was a simple one: "It gives me somethin' to do. Keeps me busy." And he certainly seems busy. Most days you can see him hauling

The Loony Lagoon gives its creator "somethin' to do . . ."

. . . and the rest of us something to look at.

gravel, raking leaves, generally sprucing up, and adding new creations to the zany theme-park-without-a-theme located behind his trailer. He's happy to show you around. But, like all true artists, he's more at ease creating the work than discussing it.

Other than the fact that it "keeps him busy," Day tends to be a bit tight-lipped on the subject of his creativity. When asked how he decides what characters to add to his menagerie, his response was a Zenlike "I just find somethin' that looks like somethin', and then I just make somethin'."

The range of "somethin's" to be found in the Loony Lagoon is eclectic, to say the least. There are homemade replicas of a stagecoach and a bowling alley (or at least a building with a big sign to that effect tacked onto the front of it). There are also numerous witches, goblins, and ghosts hanging from the trees and standing on the shore of the lagoon itself.

Well, it's not exactly a lagoon. More like a shallow backyard mudhole, if the truth be told. Hey, the Loony Lagoon ain't Disneyland, bub! But there is something undeniably, refreshingly ridiculous about the place. The whole endeavor is really nothing more or less than one man's celebration of pure fun and unbounded imagination.

Breaching wildly in the lagoon itself is a black-and-white shark with gaping jaws squaring off against a rather happy-looking muddy brown alligator. Like all Day's creations, including oddly primitive versions of several popular big-name cartoon characters, these denizens of the shallows are rendered in glossy enamel paint on sheet aluminum.

Philip Day, a man of few words and plenty of wacky ideas, obviously disdains plywood. "Plywood don't last!" he says, passionately. "Sheets of metal and logs, that's what I use!" As if building his creatures out of anything less durable would be like carving Mount Rushmore out of plaster. Hey, who am I to argue? I figure that, when a man finally finds "somethin' to do," he darn well wants to do it right.

A Monster or a Mouse?

Bath

Charlie Cahill Jr. opened his garage on the site of what is now Cahill's Tire Store in Bath, at the junction of Route 1 and the Old Bath Road, back in 1938. Charlie was quite a character in the community, and his son Skip has done a good job keeping up the family tradition. He's a hardworking guy who uses his lively sense of humor very effectively to lubricate the dull spots in the daily grind.

A few years back, Skip came up with an idea for a roadside attraction, something "a little different" that would draw passing motorists to his establishment. When you run a garage in the same location for as many years as the Cahills have, you're bound to collect a certain amount of "car junque": a used muffler here, a few spare wheels there, maybe a bit of scrap metal and a box of mismatched headlights and taillights. Hey, after a few years, it adds up. Whether the motivation was practicality (why pay somebody to lug it off?) or whimsy (more likely, in my opinion), I can't say. But Skip decided that the growing pile of automotive castoffs would make excellent raw material for a roadside "art installation."

He enlisted the talents of local artisan John Donovan and pretty much let him go where he would with the project. The result, a four-legged, long-necked, red-eyed beast about 25 feet tall, which looks like a cross between a brontosaurus and Rudolph the Red-Nosed Reindeer, is known locally as "Skip's Monster."

You can't miss the Monster partly because of the rather sinister-looking red-tinted headlight eyeballs glowing ominously from deep within the stamped steel wheel eye sockets perched on its rust-encrusted skull. "The kids like it," says Skip, as if that were some sort of explanation. When I asked him what the public reaction to his junkyard Frankenstein has been, he told me that a lot of customers get a kick out of it. But the

Skip told me he was looking for "something different." I'd say he found it!

most interesting reaction was that of one woman from Massachusetts. According to Skip, most folks think that the Monster is actually a moose or a deer. "This lady," he said, grinning, "well now, she had a different idea." According to Cahill, she came barreling off the highway as if her car were on fire, screeched to a stop, jumped out, and with a cry of rapture exclaimed, "I love it! That's the biggest mouse I've ever seen!"

Perry's Tropical Nut House

Belfast

Sadly, one of Maine's oldest and most venerated roadside attractions almost disappeared a few years back. Since opening its doors back in 1927, Perry's Tropical Nut House on coastal Route 1 has entertained, amused, or at least temporarily distracted tens of thousands of tourists on their annual migration.

I, for one, remember begging my mom to pull over at Perry's. As a matter of fact, the original Perry's Tropical Nut House, with its giant, gaudily painted menagerie of outsize animals standing around the parking area, was a near-perfect example of the "Hey, Mom! Can we stop in there and look around, pleeeeeeeze?" school of advertising.

Frankly, I don't recall being all that impressed with the actual store, you understand. What I do remember is that there was a certain third-rate P. T. Barnum ambience to the whole place. There was a fair-size herd of assorted stuffed animals, most of which, if memory serves, had apparently been worked over pretty well by a roving gang of voracious moths. There were also a lot of nuts from exotic places. I don't remember that there was much in the way of formal exhibits at Perry's, just a whole lot of dusty nuts lying around in bins and cases.

Oh yeah, Perry's Tropical Nut House was also the home of the "Giant Man-Killer Clam," a huge white clamshell with a sign indicating its murderous proclivities in life. It's pretty easy for a young boy to imagine being attacked and ripped to shreds by a snarling tiger or an angry grizzly bear, but a man-killer clam? Well, maybe. Keep in mind that I first visited Perry's, as an impressionable lad, back in the fabulous '50s, an era when ants and scorpions were laying waste to entire cities down at the drive-in every weekend. In that context, I suppose a killer clam didn't seem all that far-fetched to me at the time.

I'm happy to report that Perry's opened under new management in 1997, and owner David Sleeper seems determined to restore it to its former glory. Although many of the original exterior attractions were sent fleeing by the auctioneer's gavel, Hawthorn, the trumpeting elephant who ruled the front yard, was only relocated to Belfast center, where he now graces the Colonial Theater on High Street. But Sleeper, a fan of the original Perry's, seems determined to do the right thing and has already begun rebuilding the store's collection.

As loquacious as ever, Hawthorn now greets moviegoers in Belfast.

There's a 6-foot plush stuffed bear outside, as well as a plywood backdrop you can stick your head through while your friends snap pictures of you giggling under the message I GOT 'CRACKED' AT PERRY'S NUT HOUSE!

I, for one, am glad to see Perry's back in business. It's hard to tell just what the attraction of the original Perry's Tropical Nut House was. But if I had to guess, I'd say that the name has a lot to do with it. I think it was H. L. Mencken who once quipped, "No one ever went broke underestimating the intelligence of the American people." The ability to tell the folks back home that, while on vacation in Maine, you stopped to visit a "nut house" has got to be right up there with flatulence jokes in terms of timeless appeal.

Pink Dinosaurs Are Friendly

Belfast

Creating a truly memorable roadside attraction involves coming up with something odd, goofy, or outrageous enough to smack the eyeballs of the road-weary traveler with enough force to induce the driver to pull over and visit. With any luck, you'll come up with something nobody else has thought of.

As you'll discover elsewhere in this book, there's no shortage of outsize lobsters, fishermen, etc., populating the highways and byways of Maine. So, back in the late 1980s, when Kim Dunn and Dan Bennett decided to open their gem and mineral store in Belfast, they searched for a distinctive mascot that would stand out in the crowd of slicker-clad seamen and oversize arachnids. And, by golly, they found one.

How about a pink dinosaur? Now we're talking! It seems an unlikely totem for the Maine coast, but there is some logic behind the decision. Kim explains that the dinosaur (technically, it's the skeleton of a styracosaurus, which, according to Kim, looks more friendly, feminine, and

It's hard to believe that after all these years "Pink Floyd" is still on the road.

welcoming than its better-known cousin, the triceratops) is a symbol of antiquity and geology. (Remember those fossils you studied in high school science class?) They figured that since age and geology are what gems and minerals are all about, "Floyd" would make a fine mascot for their shop, Bennett's Gems and Jewelry.

Floyd? Oh yeah, a couple of years after it was erected, Kim and Dan held a contest to name the dinosaur. The winning name was submitted by an eight-year-old girl from Minnesota who clearly had a much better knowledge of classic British '60s–'70s arena rock than her tender years would suggest.

The original shocking pink 13-foot-long sculpture (eventually, if you sell enough Mary Kay, perhaps you could win one of these for your lawn) was painstakingly handcrafted out of pressure-treated plywood by jeweler and gem cutter Dan Bennett. It was an immediate hit. Kim says, "It pulls people right in. They can't help themselves." She also informs me that pink has been proven to be the "friendliest color," explaining that the holding cell in nearby Waldo County Jail is painted a similar color to soothe the criminal psyche while pondering one's fate.

Apparently the color wasn't quite "friendly" enough to win over a young local who wantonly decapitated the poor guy a few years back. The miscreant was eventually caught. To avoid prosecution, he agreed to assist in reattaching the ancient lizard's lopped-off cranium. Presumably, having spent some time in the company of "Pink Floyd," he ended up feeling mighty friendly about the whole thing.

True North

Big 20 Township

Quick: What's the northernmost spot in the state of Maine? If you guessed Fort Kent, as in "Kittery to Fort Kent," you would be wrong by at least 50 miles. The northernmost spot is Big 20 Township, and it's one of the most remote areas of the state as well. (Our editors encouraged us to write about areas other than the coast. Well, Big 20 is about as far away from the coast, or any part of Maine, as you can get.)

How far north is it, you ask? Well, it's closer to the North Pole than it is to the equator. At least a quarter of Canada's population lives south of it. And it is farther north than Bismarck, North Dakota, hardly a tropical locale.

It is so remote and far north that it doesn't fit on a regular page of the DeLorme *Maine Atlas and Gazetteer.* It requires a separate insert. If you look at the insert, you will notice something else: there are no state highways, or even "blue highways," in the entire township. There are only a couple of logging roads, which connect to other logging roads, and eventually they get you to the very end of Route 161 in Dickey, outside of Allagash. If you go north, and across the St. Francis River, you will get to the customs station at Estcourt in Quebec Province.

Big 20 Township is big in geography. It's actually two townships: T20 R11 and R12 WELS, which designates the Unorganized Territory—Township 20 in Ranges 11 and 12 West of the East Line of the State. (Thus, the town is not named after the bowling alley in Scarborough.)

The St. Francis River forms the boundary line of Big 20 Township, as well as that of the state—and of the United States—with the province of Quebec, Canada. This line was established by two gentlemen who never set foot in Big 20 Township: Daniel Webster, who was U.S. secretary of state, and British foreign secretary Lord Ashburton. Their eponymous treaty, signed August 9, 1842, ended the "bloodless" Aroostook War. It gave Canada some land that Mainers claimed, and it gave to the United States some land that Canadians claimed. Along with settling the boundary of Big 20, the Webster-Ashburton Treaty also settled the U.S.–Canada border out through the Great Lakes to the Lake of the Woods, limited foreign inspection of U.S. ships suspected of carrying slaves in international waters, and gave restitution to the United States for a slave ship that Britain had seized and freed the cargo. Other than those issues, we are sure its most important goal was keeping Big 20 Township in Maine's hands.

There's not much going on in Big 20. Most of the action is right across the border, where there is an Irving Paper Mill. Canadians try to sneak across the border to get cheaper tobacco products, although they might spend so much on gas and car repair that it would be less expensive just to pay the extra cost—or to quit smoking. Fewer than twenty people live in Big 20 year-round.

The biggest activity is timber harvesting, according to Don Cote, a senior enforcement investigator with the Land Use Regulation Commission's local office. Two large timber companies own a substantial amount of the land, with smaller lots owned by camp owners. There once was a gas station and a movie theater right on the boundary with Canada, but they aren't there anymore. There are just a few camps on the lakes that stride the border, but the Canadian sides of the lakes (to the east) are developed, including Beau Lake, where the muskies (not the Ed kind) are plentiful. Cote doesn't expect any major development in Big 20. And neither do we—it's just good to know that this spot is sitting there by itself at the top of the map.

Gadabout Gaddis Airport

Bingham

He was a pioneer of television, a combination of Sky King, Marlon Perkins, and, maybe, the Fugitive, because he never stayed in the same place very long. He was the nicest man you'd want to know. He was Vern Gadabout Gaddis, the Flying Fisherman.

He started out as a salesman for the Shakespeare Fishing Tackle Company, then gradually got into making films and doing a radio program about fishing (remember, there also used to be a ventriloquist on the radio). As his radio show was starting, in the late 1930s, the boys who produced the show decided that his given name, Vern, just wasn't catchy enough. "Why don't you call him 'Gadabout Gaddis'?" one of the crew said. "That's a good name for him, because every time we're looking for him, he's gaddin' about the country somewhere." In 1939 an executive from NBC asked him if he wanted to try something called television. He used his fifteen minutes to show fishing movies he had made; occasionally he demonstrated fly-casting techniques. During World War II he traveled around the world, giving demonstrations to the troops and organizing fishing expeditions. In 1963 he got his big break, when Liberty Mutual signed him to a nationwide TV series.

In the television series, you would see Gadabout Gaddis taking off in his Jeep; astute watchers would know that he was embarking from the Gadabout Gaddis Airport in Bingham, Maine. According to Wes Baker, who organizes a fly-in to honor the memory of Gaddis, the airport was built in the 1950s and acquired by Gaddis later on. Gaddis built a home on the river, where he lived for years. He died in the mid-1980s and is buried in nearby Moscow.

Gadabout said in his autobiography, "You can believe me or not, but over the last fifty-five years, I can't remember ever having spent thirty consecutive nights under one roof. I've had the hankering to roam since I could walk, to fish since I was seven." Even though he was a gadabout, he loved the town of Bingham. Baker says, "He bought things for the town and gave money to the band. Folks in town loved him."

Gadabout Gaddis is roaming on this earth no more. But the airport is still open, now owned by a white-water rafting firm. There is a runway of "2,000 feet, usable," according to Baker, but beyond that you wouldn't want to go. It doesn't get a lot of use, but there's a restaurant right at the airport, where folks fly in for breakfast.

Every year, the last week in September, there is a fly-in at the Gadabout Gaddis Airport. Baker says the first one, back in the late 1960s, was to honor the man who had done so much for the town; now it's an annual tradition. It's a beautiful time of year to see the northern Kennebec River. It's also a tribute to the Flying Fisherman, who wrote, at age seventy: "I've been lucky—tremendously lucky. Just the fact I've managed to live through seventy years and still feel as frisky as a pinto pony is proof enough of that. It's been a wonderful, wonderful life—even in the days when I didn't have any more than a nickel in my pocket. Wonderful? Mister, it's been the darndest life any three men together could ever have."

This Is Dougie Carter Country

Boothbay Harbor

Douglas "Dougie" Carter of Boothbay Harbor is pretty much everybody's idea of a Maine lobsterman straight out of central casting. He's a big rugged guy with a handsome, weather-beaten, Clint Eastwood-after-a-hard-day-in-the-saddle look about him. Behind his sandpaper-rough, Down East drawl lies a wicked yet deceptively subtle sense of humor.

Most days in the summer you can find Dougie hard at work on the waterfront. He owns his own company, The Sea Pier, a harborside lobster wharf/restaurant and wholesale/retail lobster business located on the east side of Boothbay Harbor just across the street from the Catholic church. I always try to stop in and pick up a fresh story when I'm in town. Here's just one from his vast supply.

One summer afternoon, Dougie was hard at work stacking a pile of brand-new wooden lathe–style lobster traps (the type tourists love to lug home and turn into glass-topped coffee tables and lawn ornaments) on the wharf. He was approached by a rather citified tourist who obviously thought Mr. Carter had nothing better to do than to while away the afternoon chatting with him.

"Do you s'pose I could buy one of those?" the man asked.

"I imagine," said Dougie.

"How much would you charge?"

"Oh," said Dougie, "I could let you have one of these for $75."

The tourist must have thought the price was too steep. Without so much as a thank you, he stuck his nose in the air and turned and walked down the pier, leaving Dougie to his labors. A few minutes later the man was back.

"I found a pile of old traps down on the dock over there," the tourist said. "I was wondering whether you could give me a better price on one of them."

"That's interestin'," said Dougie with a grin. "Matter of fact, I'd be happy to sell you one of those old traps. But I'll have to charge you $150 apiece for 'em." That got the tourist's attention.

"I don't get it!" the man said (never suspecting how true that statement actually was). "Why would you charge me twice as much for an old broken-down trap as you would for one of those brand-new ones?"

"That's easy," said Dougie. "These new traps here belong to me. I don't know who the hell owns them old ones!"

Douglas Carter is always good for a funny tale. But when it comes to the hard work of making a living from the sea, he takes a backseat to no man. Dougie holds the record for the trap-hauling competition at the Boothbay Harbor Fishermen's Festival. He's won this event so many times (nine) that occasionally he sits on the sidelines to give somebody else a chance. How fast is fast when it comes to lobster trap hauling? OK, here's what it involves. Participants start out standing on the dock. At the starting gun, the lobsterman and sternman race down the dock, untie the boat, start the engine, and head out into the middle of the harbor. After rounding a marker buoy, they haul, rebait, and set six traps about 10 fathoms (60 feet) apart, race back to the dock, shut down the engine, tie up the boat, and run back up the dock to the starting line. Sounds like about a half hour of work, huh? Dougie's record is two minutes and thirteen seconds.

So if you want to meet up with an authentic Maine lobsterman, you need look no farther than The Sea Pier in Boothbay Harbor. And if you decide you might want to impress your girlfriend by dickering over lobster prices with Dougie . . . well, you just go ahead and do that, sport. But, hey, don't say I never warned you.

The Sea Pier is the place where you can find out everything you ever wanted to know about lobster but were afraid to ask.

OH, TO BE A "NATIVE"

The moment you set foot in Maine for the first time, you will, like millions who came before you, undergo a subtle but significant transformation. Whereas formerly you had been simply a citizen of whatever state, province, county, town, or city you call home, upon entering Maine you will gain membership in that vast (something like 99.9 percent of the population of the planet) category of "people from away."

The opposite of being "from away," of course, is being a native. Native status has traditionally been a highly prized commodity in Maine, as illustrated by the old story of the two Maine farmers who had been neighbors on the same dirt road for more than eighty years. Well into their nineties now, everybody just assumed they were natives. Sitting on a porch one summer afternoon, the first farmer raises the issue.

"I know everybody thinks you're a native. But I heard a rumor that you're really 'from away,'" the first farmer says.

"I hate to admit it," says the second man, "but them rumors are true. I was originally born over to New Hampshire, and I was three months old before I ever set foot in the state of Maine."

Giant Fiberglass Fisherman

Boothbay Harbor

In his authentic yellow fisherman's oilskins and sou'wester hat, the giant fiberglass fisherman standing out by the parking lot entrance at Brown's Wharf in Boothbay Harbor certainly has the look of a native Mainer. But, according to Ken Brown, who owns the place, he's actually "from away."

"We got him back in 1968, from the Amish folks down in Pennsylvania," he says. Before the statue arrived (and before Maine outlawed this kind of outdoor advertising), there was a huge billboard with a painting of a fisherman pointing his thumb in the direction of the wharf. "That one was painted by 'Linc' Rockwell," says Ken. "You know, the fascist?" He's referring to local sign painter George Lincoln Rockwell III, who gained notoriety as the head of the American Nazi Party back in the '60s and met a bad end. "Linc went out of favor," Ken says dryly. "Then he went out altogether. One of his henchmen shot him." Ken adds matter-of-factly, "He did do a hell of a job on the sign, though."

Ken has had plenty of fun with the statue over the years. For a while, he told me, he had the fisherman "wired up." He had installed a microphone and a speaker system running from the base of the statue to his office, enabling the fisherman to "chat" with his admirers. The "saltiest" conversations always occurred when Ken lent the office mike to some of the real fishermen who had been in the bar whetting their whistles. This practice ended some years back.

But, according to Ken, the most unique aspect of his giant fisherman statue is only visible from a certain angle. "You gotta view him from his starboard side," he says. "It's his most attractive pose. He's very proud of it. That's why he has that big smile on his face." I'll let you figure out what's so special about this view. But I'll give you a hint: It's most likely to be fully appreciated by twelve-year-old boys and fans of Mel Brooks movies.

What's big and yellow and startles tourists?

Fat Boy Drive-In: Home of the "Whoper"

Brunswick

Before McDonald's vast worldwide "Zillions and Zillions Served" burger empire was much more than a glint in Ray Kroc's eye, there was the Fat Boy Drive-In. In fact, when John Bolinger flipped his first burger there in 1955, the massive tailfins that would forever define the fabulous '50s had barely begun to sprout from postwar fenders.

The Whoper Basket please . . . and hold the lawsuit!

Strange as it seems in twenty-first-century drive-thru America, the notion of eating a burger and fries in your car was a real novelty in the days of Brylcreme and doo-wop. In most cases, the novelty wore off almost as quickly as it had arrived. So how come the Fat Boy is still jammin' 'em in on a hot summer night?

Ken Burton, nephew of the original owner, has been running the place since 1983. He figures that the secret of his success is simple: good food, fast service, and Car Culture nostalgia. You'll find all of that at the Fat Boy for sure, but I think there's more to it than that. Maybe the real secret of the Fat Boy's seemingly endless summers is the quirky appeal of the Whoper Burger. You read that right. It's Whoper (pronounced WHOA-purr), not Whopper.

Fat Boy patty flippers had been cranking out something called a "whopper burger" for years when fast-food giant Burger King wrote to inform them that the name was spoken for. Rather than argue with the 800-pound gorilla, the folks at the Fat Boy, in true Maine fashion, simply lopped one *p* off their all-beef patty (the sign inside reads I KNEW THE STEER PERSONALLY) and kept on flipping. It's not like the discovery of penicillin or anything, but that moment of inspiration may just have been the key to the Fat Boy's booming success. After all, you can get good food at a lot of places, but the Fat Boy Drive-In on Old Bath Road between Bowdoin College and Cooks Corner is the only place in the entire world where you can pull into the parking lot, flash your lights for service, roll down your window, and tell the carhop (with a straight face) "I'll have the Whoper Burger, please."

Capturing Shared History on Film

Bucksport

When Karen Sheldon and David Weiss, founders of Northeast Historic Films in Bucksport, came to Maine from Boston back in the mid-1980s, they literally had no idea what they were getting into. "Karen and I came to Maine for an experimental year, back in 1984," says David, "to see if we could figure out something we could do that would keep us from having to go back to Boston and get 'real' jobs."

Karen and David were not the first young urbanites to try this approach, and they certainly won't be the last. But despite some pretty hefty credentials in audiovisual production back in Beantown, they found the going in Maine rather tough. "It turned out that it was pretty hard, it probably still is pretty hard, to put together a working production company up here unless you have national stature and can pull stuff in," says David.

Their big break came when Henry Nevison at the University of Maine in Orono stumbled upon a 1930s film of the last long logging operation on the Machias River. Nevison ("A one-man band up there," according to David) had the talent, but not the time, to restore the film properly. Karen and David had both, and the film restoration, the statewide screenings of the film, and a best-selling video that came later set the foundation for Northeast Historic Films.

The film, entitled *From Stump to Ship,* was shown throughout Maine. The producers expected at best maybe a few hundred folks to show up to see this cinematic curiosity of the past. Were they ever wrong! More than 1,100 people came to the first showing. "It was huge!" says David. "We had 800 people in Machias and 600 in Farmington. We showed it from Cape Porpoise to Madawaska, and thousands and thousands of people turned out." David and Karen had finally found their niche in Maine.

The Maine slogan might be "Remember at the Alamo."

The genesis of their follow-up hit, *Woodsmen and River Drivers,* is, if anything, even odder and more unlikely. "Of those thousands of people who came to see the film," says David, "some of them said, 'I've got a box of film at home that's at least as good as that.' Some of them said, 'That's *me* in the movie!'" That's right, some of the theatergoers watching *From Stump to Ship* turned out to be the very men, now in their eighties, who could be seen, flushed with youth and strength, "horsing" logs down the rapids of the Machias River right up there on the silver screen. These days, in addition to these first two films, the Northeast Historic Films catalog lists more than a hundred products.

Now housed in the Alamo Theatre, Maine's second-oldest purpose-built movie theater (erected in 1916), Northeast Historic Films is embarking upon another quest, the collection, cataloging, and archiving of home movies. That's right, Karen and David are asking Mainers to scour attics and basements in search of forgotten reels.

Home movies of Janey and Bobby in the Fourth of July parade back in '49 are really a big deal, according to David. Although Mom and Dad never set out to be great filmmakers, David says that their moving images contain much that is of historical significance for this and future generations. "If you take the Fourth of July parade, and it goes down a street that used to be lined with elms and they've all died, well, maybe you were looking at Johnny riding his bicycle when he was six. But for anybody coming down that road today, they might well be struck by how different the town looked. We have footage of Freeport that shows L.L. Bean as this little walk-up second-floor storefront." In the end, this "accidental" documentation of important historical stuff is what Northeast Historic Films is all about. "The truth of the matter is," says David, "everybody who has taken movies has captured a bit of our shared history that will just get more and more interesting and valuable as time goes on."

I was lucky enough to meet Karen and David during the first weeks of their "experimental year" in Maine back in 1984, and I'm happy to see that they found something here that would keep them from going back to Boston and getting "real" jobs.

I can also tell you that what David says of these "accidental" films is also true of the two of them. They just get more interesting and valuable as time goes on.

The "Buck" Gravestone

Bucksport

I was probably about six or seven years old when I first saw the strange markings on the large granite gravestone in Bucksport and heard the spooky tale of the Bucksport Witch. You can't miss the headstone. It's right there at the front of the cemetery on Route 1 in Bucksport. The name Buck is carved into the granite, and you can clearly see the ghostly image of what might be (if you squint just right and use a little imagination) the image of a witch's foot like a huge watermark seeping through the smooth granite. I'll guarantee you, when you've heard the tale of the phantom foot, that stain on the granite looks pretty creepy in a "cursed from beyond the grave" sort of way. Of course, the mark might just as easily be interpreted as a ghostly image of the state of Florida (upside down and backward) or a Christmas stocking or a lot of other things. But generations of locals have stamped their imprimatur on the "witch's foot" (or leg) legend, so that's what it is.

So what is the legend of the Bucksport grave marker? Ah, that's where things start to get murky. When I tried to remember the version I'd heard as a child, I could only recall that it had something to do with a woman who had been cruelly burned at the stake for allegedly practicing witchcraft back in colonial times. That seemed pretty plausible given what I'd heard of purported puritanical excesses in that department. Also, there was something in there about the woman being falsely accused, which seemed like it was par for the course. Then there was the part about Jonathan Buck, founder of the town that bears his name and apparently the poor soul whose mortal remains are even now doing the "dust to dust" bit beneath the stone. Maybe he was responsible for the rush to justice? Maybe he was falsely accused himself? Were there, perhaps, some disgruntled "Indians" involved? Something about a leg being snatched from the fire at the last minute?

The Buck stopped here—and so did the witch.

My attempts to resolve the details only deepened the mystery. I contacted Pamela Dean at the Maine Folklife Center at the University of Maine in Orono, and she faxed me some material. It soon became clear that the variety and diversity of the "ghost stories" about the image on the stone resembled the list of choices on a Chinese takeout menu, and none of them appears to have much to do with the truth. The only thing that seems clear from the historical record is that poor old Jonathan Buck (a founding father and apparently a model citizen born in 1719, well after the era of colonial witch hunts) is no more than an innocent bystander.

The rest of the characters in the various accounts include: an innocent woman with a missing leg, the village idiot, at least one witch, the witch's son, some local Indians, one or more animated talking corpses, vain attempts to chemically remove the telltale leg stain, and reopened caskets with one to three legs in them. You get the picture. It's a really good story with all sorts of spooky elements, but there are so many versions, retold so many times over the past century and a half, that nobody has any idea how the real story goes.

So here's what I'd recommend. If you have an hour to kill, perhaps you could go to Bucksport and stand in front of the Buck grave staring at the murky image with an air of wonderment and mystical detachment. Dollars to doughnuts somebody (preferably a young, gullible local child) will wander by while you're there and ask what you're looking at. At that point, you can just make up your own version of the story using some mix-and-match combination of the above-mentioned characters. This could be fun. It just goes to show that you don't have to be Stephen King to create a famous Maine ghost story. If your version contains even a smattering of the standard elements, it will merge effortlessly with all the rest of the tales floating around, and you'll have the satisfaction of knowing that you've contributed to the great Maine storytelling tradition.

All I ask is that you treat Jonathan Buck sympathetically. His only crime seems to have been living and dying before this whole story ever got started.

Road Markers to Calais

Calais

We're all used to the mile markers on the Maine turnpike and I–95. In the old days we used to measure our distance by the number of miles the billboard told us we were from Perry's Tropical Nut House in Belfast. But even before that, there were road markers, placed by a wealthy Mainer, on a stretch of what is now Route 1 outside Calais.

According to the *Bangor Daily News,* these twelve granite markers were set by James Shepherd Pike to measure the distance between his mansion in Robbinston and his office in Calais. Before odometers were in use, Pike needed a means to measure the miles. According to the article, "He tied a rag around the spoke of a carriage wheel and had a man count every time that rag came up, and as he knew the diameter of the wheel, he knew when a mile was passed, and had the place marked and a stone set up." This was probably sometime in the 1870s, after Pike had served a stint as ambassador to The Hague.

Pike used the mile distances to measure the performance of his horses—a sort of early time trial. The original stones have remained, except for mile 6, which is made from red granite, unlike the others, which are gray. The markers are listed on the National Register of Historic Places.

Maine's Treasure Trove of Trash

Coopers Mills

Elmer Wilson first opened the doors of Elmer's Trash and Treasure Barn on Route 17 in Coopers Mills back in 1975. When I questioned him as to exactly why he decided to open the doors at that particular point in time, Elmer was rather vague. One quickly deduces that Elmer has the capacity to be vague or not as it suits him. That's part of his charm, or maybe not, but either way, he's not losing any sleep worrying what you think of him, so you might just as well press on.

Having personally visited Elmer's establishment on more than one occasion, I'm going to hazard a guess. I think the reason Elmer opened his barn doors to the public back in '75 is that if he hadn't done so, they would simply have burst open of their own accord. Got a mind to paw through all this trash lookin' for treasures? You'd better clear off your calendar. There's a ton of stuff here!

What's trash and what's treasure at Elmer's is, of course, a totally subjective distinction, beauty being "in the eye of the beholder" and all that. For instance, I'm pretty sure that whoever sold Elmer the abandoned and dilapidated church steeple that sat moldering out front for a good many years was no doubt happy to be rid of it. Perhaps this now long-forgotten individual thought that he had "put one over" on poor old Elmer. Of course there's more to the story. Eventually legendary Maine painter Jamie Wyeth stopped in, and by the time he left, he'd purchased the steeple for what I'm certain was a fairly "steep" price. I can imagine that a knowing grin crossed Elmer's face about the same time that the famous Wyeth's cash crossed his palm.

That's life in the treasure game. Some you win, some you lose, and some are called on account of rain. I once stopped by and wandered around for the better part of a half hour without seeing Elmer. I plowed through moth-eaten stuffed moose heads, stacks of scratched Johnny Cash LPs, and boxes of rusty jackknives until, somewhere on the second floor, I spotted an old wooden door with some primitive, colorfully painted, hand-carved trout mounted on it. As I walked down the stairs, I heard voices in conversation. I followed the sound of the voices until I found Elmer and one of his "regulars" talking politics over coffee and tuna sandwiches. After chatting for a few minutes, I described the item and asked Elmer how much he wanted for it.

"It was on the third floor you say?" queried Elmer.

"Nope." I replied, "It was on the second floor, just inside the door at the top of the back stairs."

"Second floor, huh?" he said, scratching his chin absently and staring at the rusty woodstove just off to his left. "Was the door painted white?"

"Sure was," I said.

"Oh yeah, I know the piece you mean. I got a bunch of them a while back. I'll let you have it for $40."

Frankly, I was amazed. There must be at least 150,000 items stashed in and around Elmer's barn, and I have no doubt that within thirty seconds he'd identified the exact one I was referring to and determined a price he thought was reasonable.

I thought the price was reasonable, too, but since I was riding my motorcycle that day, I told him that I'd come back for it when I was driving a vehicle large enough to haul it off in. He didn't seem to care one way or the other, and I figured that the item wasn't going anywhere anytime soon.

That just shows you how much I know. When I called to ask about picking it up a few weeks later, his response was matter-of-fact.

"Sorry," said Elmer, "that item's been sold."

"Are you sure?" I said, amazed all over again at his seemingly photographic knowledge of the endless rambling inventory in his barn.

"Ayuh! I'm positive," said Elmer with satisfaction. "A feller come through here last week and bought the whole second floor!"

Dud Rockwell: Keeper of the Wyeth Flame

Cushing

Christina's World by Andrew Wyeth, one of the most universally recognized and admired paintings of all time, was created in Cushing, Maine, just a few minutes' drive off busy Route 1 near Thomaston. The building visible in the background, a weathered Maine farmhouse, family home of Christina and Alvaro Olsen, would be recognized at a glance by millions. So it's no wonder that a steady stream of art lovers and curiosity seekers make the pilgrimage to Cushing each year to gawk at the famous structure.

Dud's part of the landscape around here.

The Olsen House is still there all right, standing in the middle of a field, looking eerily similar to the way it looked the day Wyeth first painted it more than half a century ago. Also still standing, looking almost as weatherbeaten, yet amazingly fit and spry for his ninety-plus years, is Dudley "Dud" Rockwell. Every weekday during tourist season (Memorial Day through Columbus Day) at 2:00 P.M. sharp, Dud gives a tour of the Olsen House, complete with anecdotes about the former occupants and what seems to be an awful lot of casual inside information about the famous painter himself. How does he know all this stuff, anyway?

Despite being notoriously fond of his pipe, Dud's not blowing smoke when it comes to the Wyeths. As a matter of fact, Dudley Rockwell is about as close to being a Wyeth as you can get without benefit of DNA. "There was three of them James girls around here," he explains. "Louise was the oldest, then there was Gwen, and the youngest was Betsy.

I married the oldest one, and Andy married the youngest." Ayuh, you got it. Dud's Andrew Wyeth's brother-in-law. And it doesn't take long to figure out that he loves his "work." According to Dud, "If I didn't do it, I'd be dead. It's the only thing that keeps me going."

The Wyeths—father N. C., son Andrew, and grandson Jamie—are the closest thing to a dynasty the American art world has ever produced. Their fame has bred an understandable level of Kennedy-like reclusiveness, which in turn has bred an almost insatiable curiosity among their many admirers. Dud isn't revealing any family secrets on this tour. But he manages to give visitors a peek behind the curtain, a glimpse of the personal world of the Wyeths that most folks never see.

Far from being a mere Wyeth sycophant or a stagehand in their play, Dud's actually an incredibly interesting and talented man in his own right. His ship models are on display at the house, and the furnishings include Dudley's lovingly and expertly handcrafted replica of Alvaro's chair, made famous by one of Andrew's paintings.

And he's not a bit shy about inserting his own illustrious family background into the monologue if he senses his audience is getting restless. This has happened a few times. "A couple will come in," says Dud, "and usually it's the wife who is interested in the Wyeths." When that happens, he has a surefire technique to get hubby to sit up and take notice. "Did you ever hear of the Rockwell hardness tester?" he asks. That's clearly a change up pitch, and Dud says it usually works. A lot of them have heard of it and start asking questions. In case you are poorly informed, I'll fill you in. According to Dud, the famous Rockwell hardness tester, a device used to test the hardness of metals, was invented by his father, Stanley P. Rockwell, back in the 1920s and has been used and appreciated in metal manufacturing operations around the globe ever since—presumably by married guys with art-loving wives who wouldn't know *Christina's World* from a velvet Elvis.

DICK CURLESS, COUNTRY LEGEND

I wouldn't call Dick Curless a "quirky" character, but I'd call him a character out of the Maine mold. Here was a man from the very top of the country who made it to the top of the country charts.

Born in Fort Fairfield, Dick Curless first used his vocal powers as a disc jockey, here in New England and later on Armed Forces Radio during the Korean War, where he was known as the "Rice Paddy Ranger." His experience was the basis for his song "China Nights," according to his friend Al Hawkes.

Dick recorded some 78 rpm records in his early days. "They don't sound like the Dick Curless we think of now," says Al, "because his voice hadn't fully developed." After returning from the war, Al recorded some of Dick's early songs, including "The Streets of Laredo" and "The Foggy, Foggy Dew." And although he is now remembered for his beautiful bass/baritone voice, Dick had a terrific vocal range, including a wonderful falsetto, Al recalls. Dick Curless singing falsetto is sort of like Marshall Dodge, the Maine humorist, talking with a New Jersey accent—you wouldn't really expect it.

Dick developed his fame by appearing on Arthur Godfrey's national television show in 1957. His big song was "Nine-Pound Hammer." One version of the song was recorded in Westbrook, featuring a fifteen-year-old Lenny Breau on guitar (Breau later had a meteoric career in Nashville). Al says that when Dick was recording the part about the gas in the coal mine, Lenny either moved in his chair or released his own gas, which made the next six takes of the song impossible.

According to Al, Dick could have been a star after he appeared on the Godfrey show. "A manager wanted him to play some clubs in

New Jersey and get him ready for the big-time stage. But Dick had an oral contract to play at a joint in Bangor with a sawdust floor, so he went and did that instead."

After some success, Dick toured with Buck Owens and appeared in Branson, Missouri, and Nashville.

The big hit for Dick Curless was the truckin' anthem "Tombstone Every Mile." We Mainers were proud of that song. There are millions of songs about the heat of the South and the Mexican border, but this song is from our country, where the Haynesville Road is just "a ribbon of ice." It spoke of the hard lives of the everyday working people in the northern part of Maine and the risks they take just to make a living. This ain't no "Achy Breaky Heart"—this is the real thing, real country music. The song went near the top of the country charts in the 1960s.

There were two Maine-related men who had eye patches in the 1960s. One was the "Hathaway shirt man," whose patch was a symbol, an advertising gimmick, for the shirts produced in Waterville, Maine. The other was Dick Curless. His patch was worn because of an eye problem he had from birth, according to Al Hawkes. Like the man and his songs, it was the real thing.

Some of Dick's other hit songs were "All of Me Belongs to You," "Big Wheel Cannonball," and "Baby, Baby," which is still being played locally. "You didn't bring the songs to Dick. He'd bring them to you and would play what he liked," says Al. "Of course, that was different when he went with a big label."

Dick Curless died too young at age sixty-three. They replaced the Haynesville Road with I–95, which has a lot fewer tombstones. But his spirit is still there in the heart of every trucker who brings the spuds down from the county in the wintertime, knowing that you can "count 'em off. There'd be a tombstone every mile."

The Big Clock at the Center of Town

Danforth

The town of Danforth in northern Washington County has something in common with the towns of Guilford and Philips and with Woodfords Corner in Portland: All of these locations have big Seth Thomas clocks in public towers. The Danforth clock has something in common with nearly a hundred other clocks in Maine, and it shares a special distinction with a few dozen of those clocks. What's different is that, as this is being written, the Danforth clock is not in the same place that it had been since 1890.

"Town clocks were, at one time, a point of pride in a community, erected at great expense, and thereafter were 'everyman's pocket watch,'" says Donn Haven Lathrop of Vermont, who is a member of the National Association of Watch and Clock Collectors (NAWCC). Donn is a friend of Carroll E. Morse, now of Brunswick, who made it a lifetime ambition to document every single tower clock in the state of Maine. Morse identified and verified the clocks by town, by maker (such as Seth Thomas), and whether the clock is still running. He also managed to take a photograph of each and every tower clock, from the one at Building #13 in the Portsmouth Naval Shipyard (E. Howard, builder, ca. 1850, and still running) to the County Courthouse in Houlton (also a Howard, 1887, and still running); from Bethel in the west, with the Gould Academy tower (Electric Time, date unknown, still running) to Danforth on the Canadian border in the east. He got photos of the Union Station Tower Clock in Portland, before the tower met the wrecking ball (the clock was saved and now sits in Portland's Congress Square).

Morse observed unusual aspects of the tower clocks, such as the clock in a Down East town that had its hands permanently nailed at three o'clock (so that it was correct twice a day). He met the people who took care of the mechanical operations of these big clocks, a slowly disappearing breed. All of this was part of a national survey for the NAWCC, sort of like doing a bird count for the Audubon Society.

Donn Lathrop says that by the time World War II ended, the skills and care that were necessary to keep the clocks going had almost disappeared. Of course, people wore watches and had clocks at home. It appeared that the big tower clocks, with their tons of weights, were a quaint reminder of the days before standard time (for example, when "sun time" was used, Freeport and Portland were on different times).

Carroll Morse completed his survey in 1975, and the survey has been regularly updated since. A couple of years later, a man named Rick Balzer got tired of his career as an investment banker. He thought he would try his hand at a new career—watchmaking and clock repair. He moved to Freeport and studied the principles of tower clocks, including the "double three-legged gravity escapement" developed by Sir Edmund Becket. Because of the principles used in old clocks such as Big Ben, Balzer says, "I am able to make clocks that are more accurate than electric clocks."

That brings us back to Danforth. In 1890, when the clock was installed in the town hall, the census listed a population of 1,063. One can imagine the pride in the hearts of the town fathers (and mothers) when the 400-pound Seth Thomas mechanism was installed, and the town took its place along with the other growing agricultural communities. Over the years the economy of Danforth went elsewhere, and with it went a good portion of the population. The 2000 census listed a population of 629. The town clock was still running—but not as well as it had in the past.

"It was partly because they used oil in maintaining the gears," says Rick Balzer. Logically, one would think that lubrication would reduce the friction and make the parts last longer, but it had the opposite effect: It wore out the wheels and pinions that make the clock run like, well, clockwork. The oil collected gunk and gummed up the works. Rick and his crew of experts (including his thirty-five-year-old son, now a master clock maker, and his eight-year-old grandson apprentice, who is learning mechanical engineering) expect to restore the clock to good shape and to put it back in place by spring of 2006.

It's not as if the Danforth clock is the only thing Balzer Clockworks has to do. They are working on the "Old Maine," a 47-foot bronze tower clock for the University of Arkansas's Bill Clinton Library; they have just built the L.L. Bean clock (which plays nine to thirteen tunes, including one by Bach); they are building a clock for the Ocean Gate project in Portland; and they are doing other building and renovation projects that come to them in their role as the only clock maker in North America.

One thing that the Balzer Clockworks won't do is convert a "real" mechanical clock into an electric clock. Of course, we won't see any digital clocks coming out of Freeport either. "They aren't clocks—they are appliances," says Rick. His own timepiece preference is a Patek-Phillippe, but he admits he is never on time when going places.

Rick has enjoyed working with the town of Danforth, but he probably won't expect return business for himself—after all, the clock needs to be tuned up only every 115 years.

Maine Designer Jeans: Flash 'Em the Deer Isle Smile

Deer Isle

It seems like everybody is a clothing designer these days. When I was a kid, there were only a couple of name brands sewn on the back pocket of what were then called dungarees. Nowadays all you need is a few million bucks from the sale of your latest CD, and suddenly you're a "designer" cranking out stylish (or at least wicked baggy) denim creations that will be sucked up by mall rats as soon as they hit the shelves.

Mainers (Maine workingmen mostly) have been on the cutting edge, or at least the drooping edge, of haute couture for years. If you think this business of wearing blue jeans halfway down your butt is some new trend from New York or L.A., you must not have spent much time gazing out across the clam flats of Maine over the past several decades.

Call it Maine pride, but I think it's high time we give credit for fashion innovation where credit is due. Long before the mall rats and rap artists were doing it, Maine clam diggers had perfected the technique of wearing a pair of blue jeans in such a way as to expose large portions of their backsides to the motoring public along coastal Route 1.

These guys aren't sissies, either. They work hard bent over a clam hoe all day, and they want you to know it. You won't find any of this fashion-conscious nonsense where the undershorts are hiked up around the navel while the pants waist hovers halfway to the knee. No, sir.

You get a good gawk at a Maine clam digger's backside, and you'll see the real deal in the flesh, nothing to block your view of the gloriously upraised posterior, hung out for all (especially out-of-state rusticators) to view in all of its unadorned natural splendor.

They even have a name for it. When you see a clam digger thus clad, we hope you won't take offense. He's just flashin' you the "Deer Isle Smile."

A Real Canoe Is Priceless

Denmark

To most folks, a canoe is utilitarian but ultimately disposable. It gets dented, its paint fades, and its innards get warped or, in the case of the ubiquitous lightweight aluminum canoe, corroded. It's time for a new canoe.

But to some people, their canoe is a member of the family, a living memento of moonlit rides on the lake, fishing lessons and trips, and other summer fun long ago. For them, the damaged family member can go to rehab and reemerge, ready to make more memories. The rehab facility is in a barn on a dirt road in Denmark—the Smallboat Shop, where history is in the making, and the re-making, for wood/canvas canoes. Owners Linda Whiting and Dan Eaton have the materials, secret recipes, and craftsmanship for renovating your Old Town or Rushton. For some canoes they also have copies of the manufacturing records.

Wood/canvas canoes are descendants of the birch canoes that were used by the Native people of Maine, which differ from the "dugout" canoes of other parts of the country. They became popular in the late 1800s, when a system for mass-producing frame pieces was developed by manufacturers, who then stretched canvas over wooden ribs. The Old Town Canoe Company emerged as a leader in the manufacture of wood/canvas canoes, obtaining many of its techniques from the local Penobscots. According to Dan, wood/canvas canoes reached the height of popularity in the 1930s. After the war aluminum became popular, especially with guides, who found it to be lightweight and more resistant to damage from rocks. And, of course, outboard motors made for a new and more exciting mode of aquatic transportation. But the old wood/canvas canoes still had plenty of life left in them.

A canoe that once served a couple of generations at the summer camp comes to the rehab center at the Smallboat Shop looking faded and weary. It is stripped to its essence, including removing the old canvas and old varnish and storing the original screws. Its tips, decks, and thwarts are restored; a new layer of canvas is applied over the frame; some wood ribs are replaced; gunnels are repaired; and don't forget the loving treatment needed for the sponsons, which provide extra flotation on larger canoes. The rib work is intricate, since each rib is tapered in a special relationship with the other parts of the canoe. Dan points to a non–Old Town canoe sitting outside the shop and says its untapered ribs show a lack of "finesse."

Dan and Linda apply several coats of filler over the newly canvassed frame, which they then rub heartily with a canvas mitten—"a good exercise of a number of hours." The original filler formula called for the use of white lead. Now silica is used, but the recipe is the same as Dan got from Mr. Libby, who got it from Mr. Cyr, who got it from sources ancient and now unknown. Dan also applies a mildew-resistant material to the outside. Five coats of enamel are applied to the outside before the parts are reassembled.

Just as manicures and pedicures make for a perfect spa treatment, the rehabbing canoe receives several coats of varnish, applied to its interior. Each canoe has some special problem, identified when it is first dismantled. Each problem has a solution, provided by the craftsmen.

Some of the canoes are beyond repair, and Dan will politely reject them at the door. Most canoes accepted for work had been in the cus-

Dan and Linda will make your old canoe as good as new!

tomer's family for years. "They need to be re-canvassed every couple of generations," said Dan. Some had been in the barn or the boathouse of the family camp for many years, seeming to be past their prime. After Dan and Linda get through with them, they are so beautiful that some people don't want to put them in the water. One customer used his fully restored Old Town to decorate his business office. Each canoe comes back from rehab with a care sheet titled "Sun & Water are the Canoe's Enemy!" This is somewhat disconcerting for those who thought that a canoe is to be used out of doors and in the water.

Dan and Linda derive pleasure from near-perfect restoration, which involves meticulous attention to detail. Dan marveled, for example, at the stitching on an oar lock, made from the tip of the owner's L.L. Bean boots. Finding a serial plate, or a maker's mark, is also a cause for joy. The Old Town factory kept cards marking, with date stamps, the various stages of production for each canoe. Dan was able to access these cards over the Internet, thanks to the Old Town Company. You can look at the birth records, dating back to 1914, of the very canoe that now sits in the shop, shiny and ready for a summer on the lake (or a winter in a restaurant lobby), looking very much now as it did more than ninety years ago on the factory floor the day it was completed.

Since time appears to implode, it should be no surprise that the restoration process for a wood/canvas canoe will be lengthy. It takes more than three months of work on each canoe, from initial inspection to the drying of the enamel. There is a backlog of several months' work in the loft of the shop. Therefore, Dan advises people to expect a wait of more than a year to get their heirloom back.

All of the work doesn't come cheap, either. The price for restoration ranges from $2,000 to $2,500, more than the cost of a new fiberglass or aluminum canoe. But if this cost is stretched over a couple of generations (about forty years), it may be a worthwhile investment. Especially for a valued family member who just needed a little rehab work.

WERU Radio

Ellsworth

One of the most interesting attractions on the roadways of Maine can't be found by looking out the windshield or poring over a map. To experience the original eclectic quirkiness of this one, you need look no farther than the dashboard of your car. If you're driving along the coast between Damariscotta and Cherryfield and as far inland as I–95, just reach out and tune your FM dial to 89.9 and check out WERU (get it?) community radio. Station manager Matt Murphy refers to WERU as "listener supported and volunteer powered." Volunteer powered? That's right. This is a 15,000-watt station with more than sixty "I'm just doing this because I dig it" volunteers. Folks host shows at all hours of the day and night. Believe me, that makes for some darn interesting programming.

A lot of what goes out over the airways on WERU simply can't be heard anywhere else on the planet. Although the station owns a vast and varied music library (more than 25,000 titles and growing), the volunteers are just as apt to lug in their own stuff from home. Where else are you going to hear a show called *Talking Furniture* (a reference to the days of massive Philcos and Motorolas in the middle of the living room), where host "Rass Chicopee" turns you on to his own unlikely mix of reggae, salsa, jazz, and polka? Strange musical bedfellows indeed, but it makes you want to keep listening if only to find out what he's going to

Maine's famous for fresh air and nice waves.
WERU radio is famous for nice, fresh Maine airwaves.

play next. Or tune in some night when a local middle school teacher transforms herself into the mysterious "Paula Greatorex" and hosts her own show, *Blues, the Healer.*

WERU is to off-the-wall programming what Rush Limbaugh is to right-wing political bombast. What it boils down to is that when your neighbors are running the station, you just never know what will happen next. That's really the whole point of WERU. You just gotta tune in and find out.

Wilbur the Lobster: The Crustacean Is In

Ellsworth

Unsuspecting travelers cruising along Route 1, 5 miles east of Ellsworth in Hancock, may be startled at the sight of a huge flaming red crustacean making its way toward an old-fashioned brick open-air lobster cooker. "Wilbur the Lobster," as he has been dubbed by Ruth and Wimpy, the owners of the eatery that bears their name, has a decidedly muscle-bound look to him. If Arnold Schwarzenegger were ever reincarnated as a lobster, he'd look like this guy. It's not clear at first glance whether Wilbur is acting out a primal death wish as he crawls toward the steaming cooker or just heading for a soak in the hot tub after pumping iron in the Arachnid Gym. Either way, he's a traffic stopper, and in the tourist business that's all that counts. According to Wimpy, the monumental sculpture, a creation of local sculptor Joe Rizzo, has been a "huge" hit ever since he first crawled into their parking lot back in 1995.

Besides turning out a menu that features more than one hundred homemade items, local entrepreneurs Ruth and Wimpy (he picked up the nickname in childhood from Popeye's hamburger-gulping pal on Saturday-morning cartoons) obviously have a lot of fun with the folks who stop in. According to the couple, there's no doubt that Wilbur has been good for business. So many people stop and have their pictures taken with Wilbur that the local one-hour photo developer lives in a more or less perpetual state of déjà vu.

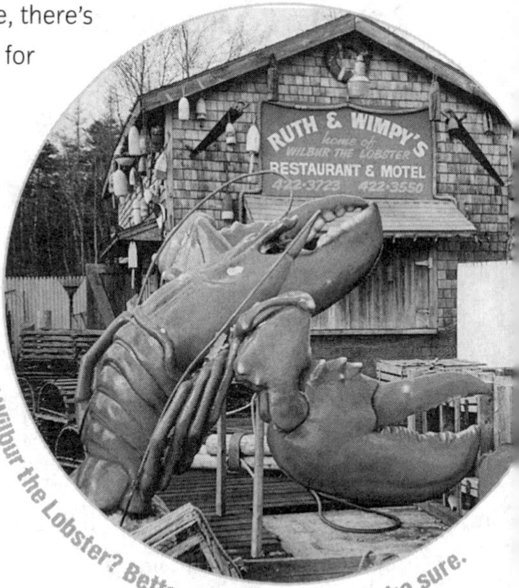

Is this the "real" Wilbur the Lobster? Better check inside to make sure.

Fortunately, after a photo op a lot of them decide to stay for lunch or dinner, and many become regular customers, bringing their friends and family back next summer.

So everybody's happy, huh?

"Well," said Wimpy, "there are some folks who get kind of upset."

"Upset about what?" I asked.

"Our sign and the postcards and so forth all say 'Ruth and Wimpy's—Home of Wilbur the Lobster.'"

"And?" I queried.

"I hate to say this," said Wimpy, "but some folks are disappointed when they come inside. They're expecting to find a live 7½-foot lobster waiting there."

Oh, I get it: "Home of Wilbur the Lobster." Where's the real Wilbur? Hey, what are ya gonna do? You give 'em a giant fiberglass lobster, and they want a live one. I guess you just can't please some people. As I was finishing up, I thought to ask Ruth and Wimpy what their last name is. "Wilbur," he said proudly. Somehow I should have known that.

Chester Greenwood, Ear Protector

Farmington

In most towns, the big celebration is sometime in the summer, when the crowds can gather outdoors in the warm weather. Not so in Farmington, where the first day of winter marks the celebration of Chester Greenwood Day. Chester Greenwood (1858–1937) was the renowned inventor of the earmuff, so winter is an appropriate time to celebrate. (Of course, if everyone wears earmuffs, it does make it hard to hear the band.)

Chester Greenwood invented his first pair of "ear protectors" at age fifteen, and he had patented the device by the time he was eighteen. He made the first pair with some pliers and coverings and linings sewed by his grandmother. Ten years later, he developed a spring-and-steel hinge, as well as machinery to manufacture the earmuffs; he continued his improvements so that the protectors could be folded to a compact size.

Chester demonstrated both his product and the process of manufacturing it at the state fair in Lewiston in 1880; he received a medal for his exhibit.

In 1883 the Chester Greenwood Company sold 30,000 pairs of ear protectors; by 1918 the figure had risen to 216,000, and by 1936 400,000 were shipped out. The first muffs were all black velvet, but by 1932 there were brighter colors, including checks and plaids.

Even without the earmuffs, Chester is recognized for some of his inventive and entrepreneurial accomplishments. In the late 1890s, he started the Franklin Telephone & Telegraph Company, and he manufactured all of the equipment. (An early telephone conversation: "Hello?" "What?" "Will you take off those earmuffs so you can hear what I'm saying?" "WHAT?") Chester also invented or developed a cotton picker (not much use for one in Franklin County), a "teakettle reinforcement," and a doughnut hook. His patented tempered steel rake sold in great quantities in the late 1930s. His company developed machinery so that other companies could make stuff like rolling pins and tool handles. Believe it or not, Chester also designed and manufactured a better mousetrap, which was in demand by local hotels and inns.

His biography notes that he regularly ran a mile without becoming out of breath, that he was a teetotaler, and that he was a regular member of the Odd Fellows.

So bring on the bands, even though there's snow in the streets, and even though we can't hear the notes because our earmuffs are in place. Let's warm our ears in honor of the man from Farmington, Chester Greenwood.

Walking and Chewing Gum

Fort Kent and Presque Isle

Northern Maine has not enjoyed the economic good times of southern Maine, with its high-paying jobs, symphonies and other "cultural" attractions and fancy coffee bars. The closing of Loring Air Force Base in Limestone and the general decline of the agricultural and lumbering industries have made life more difficult in towns along the St. John Valley. But what you will find there in abundance are dedicated, hardworking people and snow—lots of snow.

The Maine Winter Sports Center has developed world-class skiing areas in Fort Kent and Presque Isle, but they are not the trendy downhill kind. Instead these areas train and develop participants in the relatively obscure sport of biathlon skiing, and they host international events.

Biathlon skiing involves two sports—cross-country skiing and shooting. The participants ski into an area, shoot at several targets with a special biathlon rifle, and then continue on. Points are awarded based on target precision and speed in skiing. Max Saenger, vice president for Economic Development of Maine Winter Sports, says biathlon "takes a certain mentality." In order to be successful, he says, "you have to give a little on the skiing part. You can't come blazing into the target area and expect to hit the target." He says the opposing nature of the two sports builds character, helping people to balance careers later in life. This is an important skill for northern Maine, where potato farmers moonlight as taxidermists and lawyers as musicians.

Locating this schizophrenic sport in northern Maine may not be as unusual as it sounds. Of course, there is a lot of snow—and a lack of money for things like ski lifts. But culturally, the area is home to Swedes who brought cross-country skiing with them when they moved to New Sweden, Stockholm, and Caribou in the 1870s. Max Saenger says there were ancient rock carvings found in Norway of hunters on skis. And there has always been a history of winter warfare. The ski area in Fort Kent is named in honor of the 10th Mountain Division, a famed ice and snow unit that had some Maine members and fought in the Alps in World War II.

Biathlon has been an Olympic sport since 1960, and it has always been popular in Europe. The Winter Sports Center hosted a World Cup biathlon event in 2004 and will host a Junior World Championships in 2006. Visitors are expected from thirty nations, with 400 teams and members. The event is expected to draw 18,000 spectators from around the world (along with the money they spend), far in excess of the combined populations of Fort Kent and Presque Isle. The area also hosts in 2006 the U.S. National Biathlon Team trials, which will determine members of the international team. Among the participants are at least three local kids, who will be watched by friends and family. "It's like having Michael Jordan in your neighborhood and hosting an international basketball competition," says Saenger.

OK, so it's a big sport. But frankly, it doesn't really fit into Maine. After all, cross-country skiing and shooting a rifle *are* about as far apart as you can get—culturally speaking. Any self-respecting Mainer who is going out into the snowy woods with a rifle would not be caught dead on a pair of cross-country skis—he would just load up his snowmobile instead, expecting to knock off a few beer cans or rabbits for trophies. And, of course, the nature-loving, vegan purist who traverses the winter ground only on cross-country skis would rather be seen with a Bush bumper sticker on his Prius than take a gun into the woods and scare the little animals. He would rather "shoot" with a Nikon camera. If these two sports of skiin' and shootin' can be integrated into one person's ability, there may be hope that I can learn to walk and chew gum at the same time.

Sand? You Lookin' for Sand? Step Right Up!

Freeport

If you should begin to tire of the lovely green landscape and the rock-bound coast and you find yourself hankering for a change of pace, I might be able to offer some assistance. As a matter of fact, if you're anywhere near Freeport when boredom strikes, I've got just the spot for you.

There are two names for this roadside attraction. Mostly, over the years, folks have referred to it as the Desert of Maine. The more mundane (but probably more technically accurate) name, sometimes used in advertising, is Old Sand Farm. When I was a kid (back in the pre–highway beautification era, when billboards ruled the earth), there were some pretty eye-catching signs around for this peculiar roadside attraction. Mostly, as I recall, they featured a parched-looking camel, a boiling tropical sun, and a palm tree or two—not exactly lobsters and lighthouses. Actually, those signs bore more than a passing resemblance to the picture on the Camel cigarette pack. At least the artist who painted the billboards had the restraint to lose the pyramids in his version.

So how did a desert end up in the state of Maine, anyway? Interestingly enough, geologists theorize that the acres of fine beachlike sand arrived about the same time, and via the same natural delivery system, as Maine's famous rocky coast. Ayuh, when all else fails, blame it on a glacier.

This unique geological phenomenon was discovered (uncovered?) back in 1797, when the acreage was purchased by a farmer named William Tuttle. Frankly, I can't imagine Tuttle being all that thrilled to realize that, despite his best efforts, all his topsoil kept blowing away, revealing hundreds of acres of sand just underneath it. I mean, c'mon, farming in Maine in the eighteenth century was hard enough already. Eventually he gave up, and the farm was purchased by a fellow named Goldrup. Rather than fight the elements, Goldrup did what hundreds of other enterprising Americans have done with their oddities and curiosities: He put up a sign and started charging people to come and gawk. It must have been a pretty good idea. He did that for sixty-five years, and the Desert of Maine is still drawing 'em.

Now, folks visiting Maine in the summer have been known to gripe about the relative dearth of sand beaches. If you run into any, just tell 'em if they're hankerin' for sand, you know just where to look.

Freeport Big Indian (FBI)

Freeport

The FBI, or BFI (in polite company, the F is for "Freeport"), stands about 40 feet high and overlooks the highway coming from Yarmouth toward Freeport. Sources vary as to when he started his vigil, but most people recall his arriving sometime after the 1950s. At that time, the Indian looked down on a very busy two-lane Route 1; now there are four more lanes of I–95 whizzing by.

When he arrived in town, from Pennsylvania via the New Jersey turnpike, the Indian attracted a lot of attention. Many people paused just to have their picture taken with him, then stopped in at the Casco Bay Trading Post for a souvenir. This was a store that sold moccasins, duck decoys, balsam pillows, and Indian bead belts that smelled like skunks.

After the trading post folded, there was an engine repair shop and then a clothing store at the site. The advertising for the clothing store was simple: Just look for the Big Freeport Indian.

Is it just me, or does this fellow seem like he'd be happier somewhere a bit to the west of Freeport, Maine?

Built of steel rods, fiberglass, and plywood, the statue probably weighs more than a ton. No doubt the view from the top of his headdress would include the harbor at South Freeport.

Those in the more politically correct crowd don't call him FBI anymore. Instead, he's MBNA—Maine's Big Native American. Some people think he's a Passamaquoddy, but they could never explain how a sculptor from Pennsylvania would know how to carve a Passamaquoddy Indian. If you're driving through Freeport, take Route 1 for a change, and stop and say "hello."

LOBSTER BOAT RACING

The Maine lobsterman, like his western counterpart, the working cowboy, is a legendary American figure. He is, in many ways, a throwback to an earlier, simpler time, almost a mythical figure—the tough, independent workingman who routinely risks life and limb to wrest a living from a temperamental and frequently hostile environment.

To make a living at it, a lobsterman must be a combination of expert seaman, naturalist, weatherman, mechanic, engineer, and entrepreneur. It also helps if you have an independent streak as wide as the New Jersey turnpike, a body that can pump iron all day on a couple of baloney sandwiches and a thermos of coffee, a sense of humor, and a strong, competitive spirit. It's all of that stuff, especially the competitive spirit, that makes the Maine lobster boat races such a blast.

Men like Clive Farrin and Billy Hallinan, both from my hometown of Boothbay Harbor, are typical lobster boat racers. They're hardworking lobstermen year-round. But, like the legendary "thunder road" moonshiners who became the founding fathers of NASCAR stock car racing, what these fellas really like to do is make their boats go FAST! Once they've done that, they can tinker around with 'em, modify a propeller here, tweak a fuel system there, throw in a hotter camshaft, and make 'em go FASTER!!

While there are certainly purpose-built rigs out there, boats that go racing but never haul a trap, these are looked upon with disdain on the working waterfront. No, the point here isn't to have some hot-rodded rig that's too temperamental for the real world. The big challenge, the one that gets men like Billy and Clive all worked up, is to own and operate a boat that gets you where you need to go safely and reliably, fishes 600 traps, day in and day out, fair weather or foul, then proceeds to scream like a banshee, skim across the swells, and basically blow off all comers on the weekends.

There are eight major lobster boat races in Maine. The first is in Boothbay Harbor, followed by Jonesport/Beals Island, Stonington, Harpswell, Friendship, Winter Harbor, Pemaquid, and Searsport, in that order. According to Farrin, the whole Maine lobster boat racing scene started back in the 1950s on Mossebec Reach, the long, narrow body of water that separates the seaside village of Jonesport from nearby Beals Island. The Jonesport/Beals race is still held annually on Fourth of July weekend. There is a dizzying array of classes to keep track of, from outboard-powered open boats under 16 feet all the way up to the "unlimited class," with working lobster boats in excess of 40 feet whose highly modified engines regularly crank out 700 to 800 horsepower.

Perhaps you think that the whole process has gotten too professional. Well, consider this. After endless hours of preparation and thousands of dollars spent on modifications, this is what lobster boat racing really boils down to: The winner of the unlimited class at Jonesport/Beals, arguably the race of the season, walks away with a modest prize package including such coveted items as a case of motor oil and a year's subscription to the *Coastal Fisheries News.* That's it. With a cash value of maybe a couple hundred bucks in a good year, that's not what these men are after. In addition to the prizes, though, there is something far more important at stake. What keeps these fellas dreaming and scheming and turning wrenches all through the long Maine winter is just this: bragging rights. Ayuh, in the end, it all comes down to which of these men will be able to get up at the crack of dawn, slug down a cup of coffee, and head out to spend the day at the helm of "the world's fastest lobster boat." Perhaps you think that's a bit overblown. I mean, "the world's fastest"? Of course, if you'd like to discuss this with the winner, you have a perfect right to do so. Just let me know ahead of time, OK? I'd like to be there to hear the conversation.

Jules Vitali, the Father of "Styrogami"

Freeport

Millions of people all over America (you're very likely one of them) have, at one time or another, carried the graphic art of Jules Vitali around with them. Jules figures that reproductions of his designs are so common that they are very possibly "second only to paper money" in terms of the number of copies floating around out there. So how come you've never heard of this talented artist, when the sheer volume of reproductions of his work dwarfs that of all three Wyeths put together? And where can you find his stuff, anyway?

Well, for starters, try your wallet or purse or wherever else you carry your identification. You see, for more than twenty years Jules Vitali has been working for Polaroid Corporation expressing his creative spirit by designing driver's licenses.

The truth is, even creative geniuses sometimes gotta have a day job. But, after toiling nearly a quarter century in the corporate fields, Jules decided he just had to break out and give full expression to his creativity. It turns out that while cranking out those driver's licenses, Mr. Vitali had been secretly developing the revolutionary art form he calls "Styrogami." What's Styrogami? Well, it looks like delicate origami, only it's painstakingly hand-carved from a humble Styrofoam cup.

Picasso in Styrofoam?

According to Jules, "I acquired an interest in Styrofoam as a medium more than two decades ago, ironically while sipping coffee out of a cup made from same. I carry a razor-sharp jackknife called a 'peanut.'" Jules proceeded to carve the empty cup into an intricate and unique pattern, and the first piece of styrogami was born. "I've amassed over a thousand of these pieces," he explains, "each of which is as unique as a fingerprint. I carve only one or two per week, which extrapolated over a period of years, threatened to overrun my garage."

Perhaps it was simply the need to park his car indoors during the long Maine winter that finally gave Jules Vitali the motivation to break out of his safe corporate niche and head for the top of the art world. But the results have been very satisfying. Styrogami is now a registered trademark, and Vitali's work may be viewed at such respected venues as the Whitney Museum of American Art and the Chicago Center for Cultural Affairs. He has even experimented with casting some of his fabulous, delicate creations in brass and precious metals. At any rate, he's sure having fun, and people really like his new work, even if they aren't as likely to show it to state troopers as often as they would his earlier work. While other mediums are subject to degradation over the years, Vitali feels that, although delicate, his work will stand the test of time. "People tend to see stars, crowns, snowflakes, spaceships, and various other forms upon initial viewing," says the artist. "Children love them." Besides, "Life is short, Styrofoam is long."

L.L. Bean: "Start Here . . . Come Full Circle!"

Freeport

The L.L. Bean retail store in Freeport is undeniably a mecca, perhaps even *the* mecca of American retail marketing. A veritable shrine to hard work and honest value, "Bean's," as it has come to be known, is open twenty-four hours a day, seven days a week, fifty-two weeks a year. The L.L. Bean mystique draws hundreds of thousands of shoppers annually, and for good reason. High-quality innovative products like the classic Maine Hunting Shoe, backed by a no-questions-asked, money-back-if-you're-not-satisfied policy, have proven to be firm bedrock for a vast retail empire. Over the years the locals have watched in awe as the fame and success of this quintessentially Maine company grew.

We also watched in awe (and perhaps a bit of alarm) as the simple wood frame store in Freeport grew and grew. Of course, success breeds success, and L.L. Bean is nothing if not successful. So, pretty soon the original old wooden building on Main Street in Freeport was replaced by a much larger and more imposing one built of stone and metal (featuring an indoor pond stocked with brook trout). Inevitably, as floor space increased, "green space" outside the structure decreased, until nearly every inch of the surrounding acreage had been paved to provide parking for the increasing tide of eager shoppers.

The modest beginnings of a legendary retail store.

How ironic is that? Here's a company whose whole success rests on appreciation and preservation of nature, wilderness, and the outdoors, and there's hardly a blade of grass within walking distance of the place.

That all changed in the summer of 1999, when L.L. Bean held a grand opening for its latest addition. Yup, right in the middle of what seems like endless acres of free parking, there is now a "green space." That's right. They ripped up the pavement and replaced it with grass and trees and natural shade . . . right there where grass and trees and natural shade had been in the first place. L.L. Bean advertising features the slogan "Start Here . . . Go Anywhere!" In this case, perhaps the line should read "Start Here . . . Come Full Circle!"

A Bumper Crop in Freeport

Freeport

Sure, this is Freeport, Maine. But, from the moment you pull into the dirt driveway at Neil Martin's Goldenrod Garage, you're aware that this Freeport is a world away from the bustling L.L. Bean and outlet-store-dominated shopping mecca just a few minutes' drive away. You may also be excused if you find yourself thinking that, besides being in a whole different place, perhaps you've slipped through some cosmic loophole and arrived in a whole different time as well.

The old-fashioned 1940s-era gas pump out front is a tip-off. And then there are the cars. It seems like acres of 'em. Some of them are spit-shined and polished, looking eerily similar to the way they must have looked on the dealer's showroom floor back in 1957. Others aren't much more than rusting, sagging carcasses, mere shadows of automobiles cued up in the tall grass of the "back 40" like the used-car lot that time forgot.

I asked proprietor Neil Martin how this fascinating treasure trove of automobilia came to be located on a back road in Freeport. Here's how he explains it: "Philosophically, it all began in June of 1957. I bought a 1947 Pontiac 'woody' station wagon for $25, and in September of '57 I put it out on the lawn and sold it for $65 and concluded at that point I was headed down a road from which there was no turning back."

Neil was a fourteen-year-old boy when he made that first sale. Although barely into his teens, he maintains that from that point onward "the germ was planted." Like so many individuals who are "called" to a certain destiny in life, Neil Martin tried valiantly to avoid his fate, to take another path. "After graduating from Bowdoin College and taking a job in corporate America in the Boston and Rhode Island area," Neil says, "I ended up in New Hampshire." He owned and operated a restaurant at the base of Mount Cranmore for seven years. Though fairly successful in the hospitality industry, Neil continued to heed the siren song of "older autos." When he wasn't tending to his restaurant, he was buying and selling old cars.

Finally, in 1978 Neil could stand it no longer. Seduced by sedans, called by convertibles, and wooed by woodies, he abandoned any pretense of having a "straight" job. Returning to the little patch of earth where he had sold his first car back in '57, Neil hung out his shingle. He has been running Goldenrod Garage from the same location ever since.

When I spoke with Neil about the old-car business, he warmed quickly to his subject. Does he buy and sell cars outside of New England? "The farthest away I've ever sold a car was Brisbane, Australia, which is exactly halfway around the world from here. That was a '53 Cadillac." "I sell a lot of cars overseas," he continued, "I'm putting a '52 Chevy in a container today, going to Denmark."

Clearly, Neil makes a living wage with all this buying and selling. But, just as clearly, that is not his primary goal. "Since starting it full-time," says Neil, "I've been able to do that very rare thing that few people are able to do. My hobby is my vocation, and that's about as good as it gets."

But, time marches on, and some recent changes in the old-car marketplace rub a true car lover like Neil the wrong way. "Thirty years ago," he says, "people who bought old cars were 'car people.' Now, other people are buying old cars because the economy has expanded to the point where people have disposable income. A guy has a car and a guy across the street sees it and wants to have one and so forth." According to Neil, this expanding customer base "is made up of people who really don't know or appreciate what it takes to have an old car." "When the dome light doesn't work or the

Relishing rare rolling relics on the road less traveled.

door latch doesn't latch the door properly," he says with a certain amount of disdain, these folks "start lookin' around for the seven-year or 70,000-mile warranty!"

There's no question that for Neil Martin the operation of the Goldenrod Garage is far more than just a commercial enterprise. That shouldn't really surprise anyone who has seen his ads in places like *Hemmings Motor News,* the "bible" of the antique and collectable car market. For nearly thirty years he has made it clear what his real priorities are when it comes to automobiles. His ad copy reads "Goldenrod Garage: Interesting older autos talked about enthusiastically, bought, sold, traded. Since 1957."

You Can't Live on This Island

Frye Island

The town of Frye Island is composed of one island, which sits in the middle of Sebago Lake. Like some other island towns (mostly of the saltwater nature), the only way to get there is by boat. Most folks use the ferry; some people use their own craft. Long ago, one intrepid man jumped off a high rock in nearby Raymond Cape and, legend has it, swam to the island in order to escape approaching Indians. The man's name was Frye (or Frie). The rock he jumped from became known as Frye's Leap and the island Colonel Frye's Island, since the legendary biathlete had been an officer in the Revolutionary War, eventually achieving the rank of general.

In the early part of the twentieth century, a steamboat company hired a boy or man to live in a tent on the top of the rock, come out of the tent dressed as an Indian, and perform an Indian dance for the passengers of the vessel. The island itself became a summer resort, with a golf course, inns, and amenities for those "from away."

For tax if not geographic purposes, Frye Island was part of the town of Standish. The taxes went to pay for Standish schools and town services, even if many of them were not provided to the island. In the late 1990s the people of Frye Island voted to secede from Standish. As part of their agreement to secede, the town of Frye Island agreed, for a time, to join the local School Administrative District in which Standish was located. Along with this membership came the obligation to pay school taxes.

There is a hitch to all of this. Frye Island has no kids to send to school. In fact, it has no year-round residents. Not a one. "The place is locked up like a drum after the last ferry leaves," says one resident non-resident. Although there are 1,500 people in the summer (which includes a bit of spring and a bit of autumn), everyone leaves to go somewhere else for the rest of the year, whether it's to work, or to school, or to Florida. This would cut down on expenses for heat and snowplowing, one would assume.

There is a town meeting for Frye Island, at which property owners are permitted to vote. With some grumbling, the citizens have voted annually to appropriate more than $700,000 to the local School Administrative District. Recently, the town attempted to swim away from its school district obligation by suing the state. With no kids, and no prospects for any in the future, it has no need for a school. Frye Island prefers to be an island unto itself.

A-1 Diner

Gardiner

You could walk into the A-1 Diner in Gardiner and order a cheeseburger and fries or a plate of fried haddock. The question is: Why would you when the menu includes such gourmet delights as Thai crab stew, mushroom risotto, and roasted garlic penne? Why settle for liver and onions when you could be savoring the squash and apple bisque?

From the street the A-1 looks just like any other classic American diner that you can still find scattered around the country. Built in Worcester, Massachusetts, back in the 1940s, the A-1 has that lovely "railroad car" look with its art deco wood and stainless steel interior. But, as is so often the case in the state of Maine, there's more here than meets the eye.

The A-1 has been an institution in Gardiner for decades, and for the first forty years or so the menu didn't change any more than the decor. But when Michael Giberson bought the place from his father back in the late '80s, he figured it was time to shake things up a bit. After many years spent honing his culinary talents in restaurant kitchens from New York to L.A., Michael had collected plenty of exotic recipes to try out on his customers. How about some tofu, red pepper, and cashew curry, or a plate of spicy Basque chicken paella? If you haven't tried the Vietnamese bouillabaisse, you just aren't keeping up. The menu gets more ambitious each year. Of course, if you prefer a glass of chardonnay to a cup o' joe, Michael will be pleased to accommodate you.

Sure, you can get a ham sandwich here. But, why would you?

If you're concerned that things might be getting too nouveau and chichi down at the old diner, you'll be happy to know that seventy-seven-year-old Bob Newel is still back there in the kitchen, cranking out basic diner chow—homemade biscuits, pancakes, gravy, and salad dressings—just as he has been for the past fifty-two years. According to Michael, he's a real class act.

Lisa's Lobster: What a View!

Georgetown

Besides fresh-caught lobsters right on the wharf, Lisa's Lobster on Georgetown Island offers tourists and natives alike a true "slice of Maine life" experience. For starters, just finding the place is a real "you can't get there from here" proposition. Located only a few miles off Route 1, part of the "charm" of Lisa's is the trek you have to make to find it.

First you take the Georgetown Road, also known as the Five Islands Road (if you're gonna get really picky about details, it's Route 127 south), which diverges from Route 1. Just as you cross the Bath Bridge headed north (or just before you cross the bridge headed south . . . you with me so far?), drive down the road about 7 or 8 miles and, after you've crossed the third bridge, start looking for little hand-painted signs

Are we there yet?

Lisa's . . . "delight at the end of the road."

tacked up on pine trees by the side of the road. The first one I saw read LISA'S LOBSTER 7 MILES, or so I thought. The clearly amateur sign painter had painted a tiny black dot just before the 7. To confuse things a bit more, the next sign (a half mile closer) indicates that you've got another mile to go. At least the arrows point in the right direction.

As you get closer to Lisa's, the signs get more encouraging (KEEP GOING . . . YOU'RE ALMOST AT LISA'S) at about the same time the road conditions begin to deteriorate. The tar turns to rutted dirt, and the scenery starts running heavily to rusted cars, cultch-enshrouded trailers, and abandoned satellite dishes. Forget about "the way life should be"; a trip to Lisa's affords you a good gawk at the way life really is. But perseverance pays off, and before you know it, clotheslines strung from rusted Subaru carcasses give way to as charming a seaside picnic spot as you'll find on the Maine coast. And, once you get there, you can select from a menu that includes boiled lobsters, steamed and fried clams, fried scallops, fried shrimp, fried haddock, burgers, hot dogs, and french fries.

Lisa Crosby, a bouncy, energetic twenty-something entrepreneur, opened the place in the summer of '98 when she was still a senior in high school. She's been doing a land-office business ever since. She takes a philosophical view of the eyesore-laden approach to her establishment. "If they're gonna find me, they're gonna find me," she shrugs. "If not, they're gonna go somewhere else." What, and miss all this great scenery? Perish the thought!

Randy Spencer: The Singing Maine Guide

Grand Lake Stream

At this point in his career, it seems almost cruel to point out that Randy Spencer, a registered Maine guide (don't mess around with those unregistered ones, OK?), is actually "from away" (he was born in Willimantic, Connecticut, back in 1948). Despite this unfortunate accident of birth, you'd be hard-pressed to find a stronger, or more vocal, advocate for the glories of life in the Maine North Woods than Randy. He points out that his love affair with Maine began with his first visit when he was a year old and has only deepened since.

Spencer's love of Maine is matched only by his love of music. Just out of college, back in 1971, he grabbed his backpack and guitar and hitched his way around Europe, paying his way with tips tossed into his open guitar case on the streets of Athens and Rome. But the bright lights and sophistication of Europe just couldn't compete with a flickering campfire and the rustic simplicity of his favorite spot on earth, tiny Grand Lake Stream, Maine.

It was while guiding out-of-state "sports" to secret fishin' holes deep in the Maine wilderness that Randy Spencer wrote his "big hit" song. Big hit? You bet! According to Randy, in 1975 his ditty went all the way to number 1 on radio stations located "all over northern Maine, eastern

Maine, and Maritime Canada." The song that brought him stardom? Need you ask? It's called "Black Flies!" a bluesy, gritty acoustic number with the refrain "Blackflies, in your hair and in your eyes! In the old North Woods don'tcha be surprised, when you meet those devils in disguise!" The song goes on to describe these pint-size demons with an emotional intensity born of intimate knowledge of his subject matter. The radio airplay led to a tour of "some of the high places and *all* of the low ones," according to Randy. While you probably won't be seeing Randy Spencer, the singing Maine guide, on MTV anytime soon, he's not complaining. That little boy from Connecticut has grown up into a genuine legend of the Maine North Woods.

Maine's own Backwoods Balladeer of the Blackfly.

Grave of the Unknown Confederate Soldier

Gray

What can be said about a town named Gray? It is home to the Gray Water District. (Do you really want to drink "gray water"?) It has a Gray Marketplace, not quite a black market, and news items from the town are deemed "Gray Matters."

Perhaps the answer can be found at the Gray Historical Society, on the second floor of the former Pennell Institute. The society's museum features cases of memorabilia from the town, which was incorporated in 1778. It is hosted by active volunteers, Gray ladies, who are anxious to tell the historical legends of the town. One volunteer solemnly stated, "Gray has a colorful history."

Gray is the location of the first woolen mill in the United States. It was a central spot on the Portland–Lewiston Interurban Railroad (some of the rights-of-way from this road run through the fields and forests of Gray). And there is a remnant of the Civil War, located right in the center of town.

In the Civil War, Gray sent 200 of its sons into action; the Historical Society claims this was the most from any town in the state. Many boys did not come back alive, including one Lieutenant Colley. His family sent for his body, but when the casket arrived, it contained the remains of an unknown man clad in the uniform of a Confederate soldier. The uniform was, of course, gray. No one knows why this body clad in gray was sent to the town of Gray. And no one knows for certain whether the man really was a Confederate soldier or if a captured Confederate uniform was used to wrap the body.

The unknown soldier was buried in an unmarked plot in Gray Cemetery. Lieutenant Colley's body came home and was buried nearby. Gray ladies, and the Colley family, arranged for a stone to be set up for the unfortunate Reb. It's still there, marked STRANGER. In an old black-and-white photo, the grave is adorned by an American flag. Today, on Memorial Day, it has two Confederate flags, donated by the Daughters of the Confederacy. The grave, in Lane H of Gray Cemetery, is something of a shrine for Southern sympathizers. Confederate reenactors encamp near the site, which is some 1,000 miles north of the northernmost Civil War battle site. Gray merchants probably don't sing the blues about the influx of gray soldiers bringing their greenbacks.

The Civil War Monument in Gray. Does it make a Reb "blue" to be buried in Gray? Whose side was this guy on anyway?

There's another Civil War memory in Gray. The heroic monument, built in 1911 and formerly located at one end of town, was moved a few years ago to improve traffic circulation to a spot closer to the cemetery, at the intersection of Routes 26 and 100. To an untrained eye, the soldier on this monument also looks like a Southerner—maybe it's the hat. But the Gray ladies of the Historical Society say this monument is one of many similar stone soldiers built by a firm in Auburn and still to be found in northern New England towns.

After reading this story in the first edition of *Maine Curiosities,* Bertha A. Ott of Greenlawn, New York, wrote to us and reported that she had seen a statue in Kingstree, South Carolina, of a soldier who was supposed to be a Confederate, but who was depicted in a Yankee uniform. The legend in Kingstree is that the real Reb had been sent to New England. We'll have to use our gray matter to figure out where he went.

In the meantime, here's to the red, white, and blue, and the stars and bars—long may they wave o'er the green fields of Gray.

Get Naked in Maine!

Gray

You were expecting a picture of a nudist?

Get naked in Maine! Don't you just get goose pimples thinking about it? For several years in the middle of the twentieth century, sun worshipers flocked to the flesh capital of the state, Gray, to revel in their altogethers. No one I spoke to remembers much about it. One woman said her doctor treated someone there once. "For sunburn?" I asked. "The doctor didn't say," she replied.

People did know where the nudist camp had been, on Cotton Road. Today, Cotton Road doesn't even exist. It was right near the Maine turnpike. Now *that* would have been a scenic turnout. Maybe the Turnpike Authority should have placed a toll plaza there. The spot is about 2 miles south of where the highway crosses a wildlife refuge, which is south of the game preserve. With some additional work, the pike could have straddled the camp. What would the road sign look like? CAUTION—NUDE FROLICKERS?

The camp went out of business many years ago. Not very many local people attended its activities. The residents didn't cause much trouble. According to one area historian, there was really only one complaint: "We had a lot of low-flying aircraft in the vicinity."

Ken Snowden, Mr. Moose Poop

Greenville

What is it that makes great thinkers different from the rest of us? I figure it must be some inner vision, some quirk in the brain's wiring. There must be some spark of originality in the inner thought processes by which these folks are able to consider the normal everyday stuff that the rest of us just take for granted and see it in a whole new light. Think about it. Isaac Newton was certainly not the first guy to doze off in an orchard and get bonked on the head with an apple, right? But he was the first guy to discover the law of gravity as a result of having had that rude awakening.

Ken Snowden's discovery may not have had the same implications for the advancement of humankind as Newton's (we'll just have to wait and see on that one, won't we?), but in some ways his "moment of discovery" was not all that different.

According to Ken, the president and CEO of the aptly named Moose Poop Moosehead Lake Company, it was just an ordinary day a few years back when he was struck by inspiration. The world has never been quite the same since. It was a lovely fall day, and Snowden was more or less minding his own business, taking a walk in the woods.

Maybe he was temporarily distracted by the brilliance of the Maine autumn foliage, or perhaps, since it was hunting season, his eyes were scanning the trees for hunters who might not immediately notice that he had only two legs and was wearing a bright orange vest.

Whatever the reason, Ken's eyes were not on the trail ahead when the moment arrived. Stepping over a fallen log, his boot landed in a large, warm, soft substance. Glancing down, Ken instantly realized that he had accidentally placed his foot squarely in the center of a large, fresh pile of moose poop. I'm sure that this same experience has happened to hundreds, perhaps thousands, of outdoorsy types. Lesser men, I'm sure, have reacted to this experience with nothing more original than a string of expletives. But for Ken Snowden, standing nearly ankle deep in moose poop, the experience turned on the proverbial lightbulb. As he told me years later, "I stood there for a minute looking at my foot stuck in that stuff, and my first thought was, 'There's a market for this!'"

Striking while the iron was hot (or the boot still wet), Snowden collected a bit of the fresh dung and raced back home to his workshop to investigate the possibilities. A short while later he emerged triumphant.

Scoff all you want. I'm sure Ken is laughing, too, or at least smiling, all the way to the bank. You see, it turns out that there was indeed "a market for this." The Moose Poop Moosehead Lake Company is currently shipping moose poop earrings, tie tacks, refrigerator magnets, and a half dozen other genuine Maine moose poop products all over the country. Ken tells me that he has sold Maine moose poop jewelry throughout the South and the mid-Atlantic states. He even has customers in California. Hey, you just can't argue with success. I doubt if this stuff will ever appear in the Tiffany store on Fifth Avenue. But apparently lots of folks are eager to shell out their hard-earned cash for a chance to have their bodies adorned with the natural beauty that can only come from jewelry lovingly handcrafted from tiny chunks of authentic moose poop.

PERCIVAL BAXTER FUN FACTS

Percival P. Baxter (1876–1969) was a monumental Mainer. Like his beloved Mount Katahdin, he was larger than life. We all know that he gave to the people of Maine the mountain and its surrounding land, to be enjoyed in its forever wild state. But you might not know the following:

1. As a student at Bowdoin College, he brought his dog, Deke, to classes with him. One time his dog vomited in class and received the sympathy of Baxter's professor.

2. As a young attorney, he set up a sting operation to foil a bribery effort in 1900.

3. While Baxter was governor (1921–1924), the president of the Maine Central Railroad gave Baxter's dog a first-class human passenger ticket on the line.

4. When his irish setter, Garry Owen, died, Governor Baxter ordered the flags on all state office buildings to be lowered to half-staff in mourning, saying that the faithfulness of his pet stood in sharp contrast to the fickle nature of humans. Some of his dogs were buried on the grounds of the Baxter School for the Deaf, with a tombstone bigger than most stones that mark human remains.

5. In the 1920s Baxter dedicated the Soldiers and Sailors Monument in Kittery. What no one knew was that he had hidden a letter underneath the statue, talking about public service and about his

unfulfilled love life (he was never married). The letter was uncovered in the spring of 2001 during renovations to the statue. It was read by the current governor, then placed back in its container.

6. In 1936 he proposed (although not publicly) that Maine secede from the United States and join Canada, and that the Kittery Bridge have a sign that read LEAVING U.S., ENTERING MAINE. Among the improvements resulting from a Maine–Canada link: "Portland would become a maritime metropolis" and "Bath would turn out ships for the British navy."

7. A bust of Baxter was placed, in 1956, in the Hall of Flags in the statehouse, along with war memorabilia. A state senator from the district where Baxter State Park was located tried to have the bust removed. His efforts failed, and the senator was not reelected. The bust was damaged by a vandal in 1996. No one knew why. "If it had been [former governor John] McKernan, I would have given him a hand," one capitol observer said. As a result of a private fund-raising effort, the bust was repaired and sits, good as new, in its old location.

8. When he died, he left more money for the operation of Baxter State Park, in an effort to maintain the independence of the mountain and the park.

Besides the legacy of the splendid beauty of Katahdin, what other secrets has Percy left for us?

What Do You Say to a Moose?

Greenville

When you've got lemons, you make lemonade. When you've got moose, you make . . . a tourist attraction. The Moosehead Lake Region is developing into a major moose market. Stephanie Gardiner, from the Moosehead Region Chamber of Commerce, says that eight out of ten people coming into the chamber's office ask where they can go to see a moose. Many of these people insist that the moose are all in one spot. Some of the more zoologically challenged have asked, "When do the deer turn into moose?"

It's not uncommon for moose to wander the streets of Greenville, a la the TV show *Northern Exposure*. They are everywhere, especially on the highways at night, when they enjoy jousting with automobiles.

The region capitalizes on its moose connection. For instance there's Moosemania, a festival in early summer, which features the Tour de Moose bicycle race. One spot serves Moosehead Gingerbread. The Black Frog Restaurant serves moose balls (don't ask). Stephanie was not sure whether any restaurant served mousse for dessert.

All is not perfect in moose land, however. There are two types of people who want to see moose: those who just want to see them as part of a nature experience, and those who want to hunt them and eat them. Peak foliage time often coincides with the one-week moose-hunting season. As a result, leaf peepers can find themselves looking at cars and trucks draped with dead moose. Both groups bring money into the region, but coexistence may be a problem.

In 2001 an effort was made to accommodate the peepers and the shooters. One week was set aside for hunting moose and another for looking at them. This tradition has continued—hopefully with the viewing part preceding the shooting part. But there are concerted efforts to expand the length of the moose season and the number permitted to be taken.

So what do you say to a moose? Stephanie Gardiner says, "Just leave 'em alone." Some folks in Greenville, when encountering a moose, go right up to him and whisper in his ear, "Thanks, big guy."

Abbot Vaughn Meader: That's Show Biz, Buddy

Hallowell

Quick, what's the fastest-selling recording in history? Something by The Beatles perhaps? Elvis? Alvin and the Chipmunks? You're not even close. I'll give you a hint. The album was recorded in New York City in October 1962 by a Maine man, and it sold four million copies in four weeks. How good is that? Well, consider that the previous all-time best-seller, the sound track of *My Fair Lady,* took a full year to sell that many copies. In case you haven't guessed, the record I'm referring to is *The First Family Album,* a parody of the Kennedys' White House life at the height of Camelot.

The meteoric rise and precipitous crash of Abbot Vaughn Meader's comedy career is one of the strangest and most gut-wrenching tales in show biz history. Meader, born in Waterville in 1936, was working his political comedy/parody act in New York clubs when he hit pay dirt. He was onstage, fishing for a laugh, when he ad-libbed a bit of Kennedyesque "Let me say this about that" dialogue using his native Maine accent as a basis for the universally recognized Kennedy Bahston brogue. The audience went wild.

Meader refined the skit to include other Kennedys and current political figures, and in October of 1962 (ironically on the same evening that the president went on network TV to give his "Cuban Missile Crisis" speech) he recorded his trademark parody album of the Kennedys supposed White House life. Public response to the album was huge. Sitting in a hotel room in Detroit, barely a month after the recording session, Meader began to realize the meaning of fame. In a span of a few minutes he fielded calls from the *New York Times, Life* magazine, and the *Ed Sullivan Show.* Suddenly hot as a pistol, Meader spent one dizzying year riding a rocket ship to stardom. Within twelve months the album had sold nearly eight million copies, and Meader seemed destined to become one of the great comedians of the twentieth century.

But that was not to be. Where were you when you heard the news? Meader was in a taxi in Milwaukee on November 22, 1963, when the driver turned and asked, "Did you hear about the president getting shot in Dallas?" Assuming he had simply been recognized by one of his millions of fans, Meader replied, "No. How does it go?" Before the driver could explain, the radio announcer read the latest bulletin on Kennedy's assassination, and Meader's rocket ship crash-landed with a thunderous explosion. Shortly after that, comedian Lenny Bruce quipped, "They put two graves in Arlington: one for John Kennedy and one for Vaughn Meader."

Thankfully, Meader didn't die that day. But, in many ways, his career did. Despite pleas from his legions of fans, Meader kept his vow never to resurrect the Kennedy parody act. (A grateful Bobby Kennedy wrote Meader a note thanking him for his sensitivity in volunteering to cease doing his JFK impression after the president's death.)

Meader's last years were spent mostly out of the limelight. He divided his time between homes in Maine and Florida and continued to enjoy performing, notably at a restaurant in Hallowell where he was the kitchen manager. He made several more recordings (friends and fans agree that the comic was an extremely talented musician with a phenomenal knack for snappy, off-the-cuff parody songwriting), though none of his later projects approached the commercial success of *The First Family Album.* Vaughn Meader passed away on October 29, 2004, having learned firsthand that the spotlight of fame can inflict near-fatal burns. As any fan of the Broadway musical *Camelot* (Jackie and JFK were among them) can tell you, it's a wonderfully entertaining show. But the ending is a real tearjerker.

A Chain Saw Michelangelo

Hancock

Examples of chain saw sculpture, typically rough-hewn bears or lobstermen or moose fashioned from great slabs of wood by chain saw-wielding "artists," are fairly common in Maine. You can see them all painted up in bright primary colors in the parking lots of restaurants and gift shops or gradually acquiring a natural patina on lawns and in public parks.

Frankly, until I met Ray Murphy at his roadside chain saw sculpture emporium on Route 1 in Hancock, I just assumed that the folks who make this stuff were all pretty much alike. Boy, did he ever set me straight on that one!

Ray Murphy is the self-proclaimed "World's Original Chain Saw Sculptor," and that's not an idle boast. According to Ray, he personally invented the art form back in 1953, when, as an eleven-year-old boy he used his chain

The trouble with fame is that you spend half your time posing for pictures with fans.

saw to inscribe a series of four-letter words on the woodpile behind his daddy's shed.

As with all great discoveries—the wheel, electricity, the splitting of the atom—conditions had to be just right. According to Ray, the previous year "a man named Fox" had invented a new type of chain saw blade that, unlike the old-style blades, could be sharpened to an incredibly fine edge, thus allowing Ray to work in the degree of detail necessary for sculpting logs.

If you think maybe Ray is overstating his position in the chain saw sculpting hierarchy, a visit to his bus/chain saw sculpting museum, which is parked right on the lot behind the sculptures, should convince even the most hard-core skeptic. Inside the bus, a 1960 GM model with a million miles on the odometer, most of them put there by Ray himself, you will find ample evidence that he is exactly who he says he is: the World's Original (and greatest) Chain Saw Sculptor.

As proof of his claims, Ray points out that his work is currently on display in all the Ripley's Believe It or Not! museums worldwide. He is officially listed with Ripley's as the Only Man in the World who can accomplish the following seven mind-boggling feats of chain saw artistry.

Using only a standard-issue, nonmodified chain saw, Ray Murphy can

1. Carve the entire alphabet on a regular number 2 pencil.
2. Carve your name on a belt buckle while you're wearing it.
3. Carve a chair (back, seat, and four legs) out of a block of wood in ten seconds.
4. Carve a sculpture using two chain saws at the same time.

Come on, honey. It'll look great in the den.

5. Carve *two* sculptures simultaneously using a chain saw in each hand.
6. Carve his name with a chain saw on the head of a wooden kitchen match without lighting the match.
7. Using only a chain saw, carve the numbers 1 through 10 on a wooden toothpick.

That last one is the topper, what Ray calls "the ultimate." He claims that this is "as near impossible as it gets" and says even he, the World's Original Chain Saw Sculptor, needs two solid weeks of intensive training before attempting it.

Ray has carved more than 50,000 chain saw sculptures so far, and he shows no signs of slowing down. He's a living, breathing, sawdust-blowin'-in-the-wind example of a true Maine roadside attraction.

IT'S OK TO BE "FROM AWAY"

While visiting the state of Maine, you're likely to hear quite a lot about PFAs (people "from away"). Occasionally, the comments will be mean-spirited, but that's a rarity. For the most part, the term is pretty innocuous.

So who are these folks, and why is it so important that they be identified? Well, I don't exactly know how to break this to you, but, basically, if you weren't actually born in the state, you are a PFA. PFAs fall into one of three categories:

1. Tourists: These are folks who stop by for only a few days, generally during the summer months.

2. Summer People: The old-fashioned term for these folks was "the summer complaint," but you don't hear that much these days.

3. Transplants: People who have moved to Maine "from away" and now live here year-round.

The biggest problem most folks have involves people in category 3. I mean, they live here year-round, right? They pay taxes here. Their kids go to school here. How come they aren't full-fledged Mainers? This is the part that bugs PFAs the most. I'll get to that in a minute.

Meanwhile, to better understand the PFA phenomenon, you'll need a little background material. Historically, Maine has pretty much always been a relatively poor, relatively isolated state (we are the only state in the nation that borders only one other state). The winters here are long and cold. The summers are marvelous, but brief. Basically, we figure it takes a certain amount of toughness to make it here over the long haul (and Mainers definitely care about the Long Haul).

On the other hand, Maine, especially in the summer, has always been a big vacation spot. But keep in mind, while all the visitors are here enjoying "Vacationland," the natives are working. After Labor Day? We're still working. In the middle of the long, dark Maine winter? Ayuh, still working, often at two or three jobs just to make ends meet (which we call "gettin' by"). So perhaps there's a little resentment at work here. The old-timers had a saying that expresses it pretty well: "If you can't take the winters, you don't deserve the summers!"

OK, maybe that explains the attitude regarding "summah folks." But what about those who do move here and stay year-round? Aren't they entitled to full native status? Well, yes and no. Actually, they are. And most of them will admit that they are not subjected to any serious discrimination and are well accepted in the community. So why are they still referred to as being "from away"? I think it's just a matter of Maine pride mixed with a big dose of traditional Yankee contrariness.

Perhaps it all boils down to the fact that, by maintaining a strict line based solely on what is generally an accident of birth (though pregnant women have been known to go to some lengths to get back to Maine so that a child can be born within the state's borders), Mainers are simply holding on tenaciously to the one thing that cannot be acquired with all the wealth, power, education, begging, wishing, hoping, or arm twisting: a Maine birth certificate.

Bailey Island Bridge

Harpswell

About 14 miles from Cooks Corner in Brunswick is a bridge, which, because of its status as a civil engineering landmark, is listed on the National Register of Historic Places. It's the cribstone bridge that connects Orr's Island with Bailey Island on Route 24. The unique design of the bridge came about because of the way the tide works. Granite slabs were stacked in a crib, or cellular, fashion so that the tides could ebb and flow, back and forth. The slabs are strong enough to withstand the buffeting of winds and waves. At least, they have been since the late 1920s. The roadway was built on the cribs, and a sidewalk was added in 1951, according to the Department of Transportation.

Unlike a bridge over a river or a gorge, this bridge connected the rest of the world with an isolated spot, and it had a major impact on life. The prebridge residents of Bailey Island were not genteel summer folk rusticating by the seashore. They were fishermen, and the winters on an isolated island were long. "There were a lot of Johnsons on that island," says a member of the historical society. No doubt.

The town of Harpswell didn't want to pay for a bridge to Bailey, but the state chipped in enough funds to build it. The bridge brought in the gift shops and summer folks—and it put a feather in the cap of the engineers at the State Highway Department.

The Buzz That Just Won't Go Away

Harpswell

Martinis may have been the big deal in the fabulous '50s, but here in the twenty-first century it seems more and more apparent that caffeine is becoming America's drug of choice. Suddenly, there seems to be a coffeehouse on every street corner, and people actually base their new vehicle-purchasing decisions on the number of cup holders available per occupant.

Brett Johnson of Harpswell is nothing if not an astute observer of pop culture. A lifelong entrepreneur, Brett has come up with a uniquely Maine response to the nation's seemingly limitless thirst for strong, hot java. Brett's brew is called Maine Black Fly Roast, and the tagline, "For the buzz that just won't go away," obviously gets people's attention. The stuff is "flying" off the shelves faster than bug spray in the Allagash Wilderness. "We sell literally tons of it to some wonderful registered Maine guides," says Brett. And, he notes proudly, "We are the 'official coffee' of the Maine Blackfly Breeders Association." Brett sells Maine Black Fly Roast throughout New England, in the Adirondacks, and through mail-order catalogs as well. "L.L. Bean carries our product," says Brett, "and a great little catalog out of Glens Falls, New York, called The Pack Basket."

For those caffeine lovers who find themselves bungee jumping into the Grand Canyon, driving the Indy 500, or pursuing some other activity not conducive to slurping java from a cup, take heart. Brett has a new product for folks like you. "We call 'em Black Fly Bites," he says enthusiastically. "They're dark chocolate–covered coffee beans you can chew anywhere, anytime."

Mmmm, be sure to bring some along the next time you're planning a quick jog to the top of Mount Katahdin.

He even gets unsolicited fan mail attesting to the potency of his brew. The store at Mount Blue State Park serves and sells Maine Black Fly Roast. A satisfied customer e-mailed Brett extolling the virtues of the coffee with the continual kick. "After just one cup," she wrote, "I got so 'buzzed' that I cleaned the guy's store for him!"

That last one really got me thinking. If Maine Black Fly Roast really does have *that* effect on people who drink it, maybe I ought to start serving it to guests who drop by my place.

THE BIGGEST FISH

One fine day in 1959, Mrs. Earl Small landed a white perch in Messalonskee Lake. It weighed 4 pounds, 10 ounces. It still stands as the Maine record for a white perch, according to Landbigfish.com. Some of the other common big fish of record include a 22-pound, 8-ounce landlocked salmon caught at Sebago Lake in 1907, an 11-pound, 10-ounce largemouth bass caught at Moose Pond in 1968, and brown trout at 23 pounds, 5 ounces caught at Square Pond in 1996.

But there are also records for fish that are not so familiar. A black crappie at 3 pounds, 4 ounces in Sibley Pond, a splake weighing in a 10 pounds, 3 ounces caught in Mt. Vernon in 1993, and a cusk weighing 33 pounds, 4 ounces caught at Perkins Cove in Ogunquit in 2002. Allen Dufour caught a muskie (muskellunge) weighing 26 pounds, 8 ounces at Glazier Lake, after a filibuster on the fishing line.

What do you do with a fish that big anyway? Like the 31 pound, 8-ounce lake trout landed in 1958 by Hollis Grindle. Either he fed the entire neighborhood with it or kept it in his freezer until his wife told him it was either that fish or her, and he said, "I'm thinking." And unlike the tasty 4 pound, 10-ounce white perch caught by Mrs. Small, what are you gonna do with the yellow perch, weighing 1 pound, 10 ounces caught at Worthley Pond in 1989? It's too little to mount, too bony to eat. So you do what the best fishermen do—you throw it back. But you hope no one else catches it, because then they will have the record and their fifteen minutes of fame.

The "Junque" Man with a Curator's Soul

Harrington

There are actually some world-class museums in the state of Maine; the Maine Maritime Museum in Bath and the Farnsworth in Rockland come to mind. But the Down East Museum of Natural History, located along an otherwise deserted stretch of Route 1 in the town of Harrington in rural Washington County, is in a class by itself. Class? Well, that's not exactly the first word that pops into your mind when you first clap eyes on the place. Frankly, junkyard would be a lot closer to the mark.

And a sprawling heap it is, too. So what's with the professionally lettered sign out front announcing to all and sundry that they've finally arrived at the Down East Museum of Natural History? Is this some sort of joke? That's what I thought, until I took the time to discuss the genesis of the "museum" with its founder, Jerry Blackburn.

Everything you need . . .

. . . and a whole lotta stuff you got no use for.

Jerry moved to Maine from Sioux City, Iowa, back in 1983 and opened his roadside attraction about two years later. What it is, is "the biggest little acre in Washington County," says Jerry proudly, jammed full of "preowned" merchandise. He claims that if you take the time to paw through all the stuff he's got, you'd find "everything you could ever dream of . . . and mostly two or three of 'em!" The "exhibits" on display at this museum include tired fifth-hand appliances, hubcaps, kitschy living room accessories, and chipped, faded old road signs.

So the Natural History Museum sign must be just a gag, right, poking fun at rural Maine poverty? Actually and surprisingly, the answer is no. You see, it turns out that Jerry is actually a sensitive, thoughtful guy who pays very careful attention to the stream of odds and ends that flow through the place. He may be a transplant from Iowa, but it's soon obvious he really cares about preserving every scrap of genuine Maine history he runs across. Jerry Blackburn is in fact a "junque" man with a curator's soul. For the doubters among you, I offer the following evidence.

While we were talking, Jerry fished out a section of wooden beam he had salvaged from the old Centerville schoolhouse. On the beam this poem had been penned in the careful, flowing penmanship of an earlier, simpler time:

This is a fine frame

It's built with strength and might

It stands on a hill

Of beauty and delight

O' may it long stand tall, for the owner's good

And every year be filled with school days good

It will be a fine building

With plenty of room

May fire or tempest

Never it consume

—M. D. Chandler, May 1, 1858

He's not selling that piece of history, no sir. "That," he says, "is part of the museum."

A LOVE FOR LAWN ORNAMENTS

Mainers take their outside decorating seriously. Some folks worry all winter long about how they're going to place their objects in the front yard to make the appropriate statement. The art of "lawnahge" has grown through the years, and it has expanded across traditional socioeconomic strata.

Take the flamingo—please! This humble plastic bird was often the staple of lawn ornamentation. The coming of spring used to be heralded by the blooming of the pink flamingos in the window of J.J. Newberry's on Main Street. Flamingos, like most plastic lawn ornaments, had a certain charm for a certain class of people. But flamingos became the ornament of choice for the "slumming it" set. Now the plastic birds adorn Cape Elizabeth yards and professional buildings. The antiestablishment theme of lawn ornaments has been co-opted by the establishment, or at least by their yuppie children.

Here are some others:

- Bent-over Ladies. Now, there is an ornament lacking political correctness. You don't see many of them, mostly because the people who buy lawn ornaments are women and they'd rather not have another fat woman bent over in their yard.
- Gazing Balls. These are anything from high end to cheapo. The expensive ones, handcrafted and delicate, look exactly like the machine-made ones that you can get at Wal-Mart.
- Cartoon Characters. These will usually be found in the yards of people who also have satellite dishes, or people who spend more on their large-screen TVs than on, say, encyclopedias for the kids. The Warner Brothers cartoon characters, like Daffy Duck, Bugs Bunny, and Taz, the Tasmanian devil, are sold at every roadside ornament stand, but not, for some strange reason, at Warner Brothers stores in malls.

- Whirligigs. We do get a lot of wind at times here in Maine, especially in the winter. You don't need a wind-speed gauge, though, if you can see how fast the wings on your bird are a-spinning. You should never put WD40 or any kind of lubricant on the wings of whirligigs, because it might confuse them and it would give you a false idea of the wind speed.
- Metallic Figures. These are often cut into the shape of a moose or a guy sitting there smoking a pipe. If your yard is big enough, one of these turned just right will give a driver coming down the highway a moment of thought.
- Exploded Tires, Painted White. Some folks think these are too "southern," since you see a lot of them when you go to Florida. Of course, the reason you see them in Florida is that someone from Maine brought them there in the first place. The tires are good for recycling, they make good planters, and they are always in good taste.
- Washing Machines. This is one of the best types of lawn ornaments. It takes up a lot of space, and if you have more than one on your lawn, people aren't going to bother you too much.

Now here's a lawn ornament to crow about.

The Eternal Leak

Houlton

Citizens of Aroostook County are a hardy breed, not much given to complaining. They're mostly hardworking farmers making the best of the hardscrabble economy, short growing season, and long, cold Maine winter. They're well aware that the big boom in tourism that brings an annual shot of seasonal prosperity to much of the coast has long since faded to a distant echo by the time you pull into Houlton several hours north of the nearest lighthouse or lobster shack.

But, as I've said, County folks just aren't complainers. Given half a chance, they'll put the best spin on most any situation and keep on going. While they'll readily admit that most of the big tourist attractions are "down south," they don't cry over spilled milk. They just crow over spilled water . . . or leaking water . . . or whatever sort of water it is that leaks, spills, or pours twenty-four hours a day from one of Aroostook County's few genuine tourist attractions. As any schoolchild in Houlton will tell you, the attraction I'm referring to is the famous *Boy with a Leaking Boot* statue in Pierce Park at the junction of Main and Military Streets in downtown Houlton.

The statue, which also serves as a fresh drinking water fountain, was cast in zinc at J. W. Fiske Iron Works in New York and erected in Houlton in 1916. It depicts a young lad who has apparently just discovered a leak in his boot. Having removed the boot, he holds it aloft, a slightly bemused expression on his face, as if to say to the casual onlooker, "Oh my goodness! Look what happened! My boot has a leak in it, and it has been leaking like this ever since 1916!" That's it. No secret meaning or hidden message, no historical significance that anybody can recall. In fact, nobody in Houlton seems to know or care who the boy is or what happened to the boot or why for a century now it's been leaking like a sieve.

If your travels take you to Houlton between late October and mid-April, you'll have an opportunity to visit the famous statue in what Houlton police chief Dan Soucy refers to as his "winter quarters." "We keep him right here in the lobby of the police station all winter," says Chief Soucy, adding with a smile, "He likes it here! He gets decorated for the holidays with a Santa hat and red bunting. The works!"

Since it's been estimated that more than 10,000 photos of the Boy with the Boot statue are snapped annually, perhaps there is a message here after all, one that reflects the indomitable Aroostook spirit. Maybe the statue is saying, "Don't shy away from life's difficulties! Hold 'em right up there and take a good, long look at 'em!" If you do that long enough, who knows? Some tourists might eventually stop by to see what you're up to.

How's this for a catchy slogan? "Visit Houlton, Maine! It's worth a trip . . . to watch it drip!"

GENERIC TOWNS

A lot of us have places in our homes or offices that we call "unorganized territory." But the biggest contiguous unorganized territory east of the Mississippi River is in the state of Maine. It's called the Unorganized Territory, strangely enough, and it comprises about half of the state's geography, mostly in the north and west. Less than 1 percent of Maine's population lives in this area, but it's where you will find most of the state's trees, moose, unspoiled waterfront, and endangered species.

The territory consists of "townships" and "plantations." The townships were laid out in grids, or ranges, by surveyors sitting in warm, cozy offices back when Maine was part of Massachusetts. If you look at the northwest corner of the state, you will see towns with names like "T8 R5 WELS," which translates into Township 8, Range 5, West of the East Line of the State. Other ranges have names like Bingham's Kennebec Purchase, Eastern Division, Northern Division, East and West of the Kennebec River. In addition to being numbered, some townships have "town names," like Upper Cupsuptic, which is T4 R4 WBKP (Township 4, Range 4, West of Bingham's Kennebec Purchase).

When the townships were laid out, some were given to schools or colleges as a means of raising money. So we can find the Hopkins Academy Grant in Penobscot County, the Bowdoin College East and West Grants in Piscataquis County, and the Sandwich Academy Grants (they don't say what kind of sandwiches were made—perhaps a pinecone rollup?).

When the surveyor's range ran out of neat-looking, square townships on his map, the little piece left over was called a Gore, so we have Misery Gore, Moxie Gore, Powers Gore, and a score more of gores galore. A large number of coastal islands are not part of any town; their few isolated inhabitants are also part of the Unorganized Territory.

What makes these townships "unorganized?" For one thing, nobody lives there to speak of, and governments are just not practical. Some of the unorganized townships were once towns, but they faded away and became "deorganized." The little town of Madrid, in Franklin County, became a township just a few years back. Benedicta, in Aroostook County, deorganized in 1987. Not all of the townships are contiguous; sometimes an unorganized town will sit as an island amid organized municipalities.

When there are enough people to sort of organize a town, but not enough to run the darn thing, the intermediate level of government is called a "plantation." These organizations have some town officers and a town meeting, but many of their functions are taken over by the state or county.

The land in the Unorganized Territory is owned in large sections, sometimes hundreds of thousands of acres. The big landowners were, up until a few years ago, paper companies and companies that harvested wood to sell to the paper companies. Some companies own or have owned entire 36-square-mile townships. Lately, some of the larger holdings have been split up, and the land has been sold to individuals or to companies that want to develop recreational property. (Some people own just a quarter of an acre for their hunting camps.) Other new landowners want to preserve the land, perhaps even creating a North Woods National Park.

CONTINUED

What do you get for all of this "unorganization"? No, it isn't a paradise for anarchists or extreme libertarians. There are state agencies that run things. A small office in the Department of Revenue collects taxes from the inhabitants. The biggest government function is provided by the Land Use Regulation Commission. LURC is the planning and zoning agency for all of the unorganized townships and plantations. It is often faced with making decisions on whether to permit large-scale developments of second homes; it also can decide where an individual has to locate the septic system for his hunting camp. LURC has halted developments based on the presence of a little mouselike creature called the yellow-nosed vole. It gets heat from local folks, who make their money from working in the woods, and from tree huggers, who don't want anything to change in the largest remaining unspoiled tract in the eastern United States.

Schools for the few children who reside in the area are administered both in Augusta, at the Department of Education, and in local School Administrative Districts. Counties keep the roads in repair and provide some law-enforcement service. And the biggest functions of local government, registering your car and getting a dog license, are delegated to the nearest "real" town. So if you live in Molunkus, TA RF WELS, you have to go over to Mattawamkeag to get Rover's tags.

Just like the desk in my office, don't expect things to get organized any time soon. The overall population has gone down in the unorganized townships and plantations. Towns with marginal existence are giving more serious consideration to joining the ranks of the deorganized. And most Mainers probably enjoy the fact that half of the state is unorganized. They might even ask, "Which half?"

Aroostook Bumper Sticker: Not like Massachusetts

Houlton

Some bumper stickers only make sense, or at least make *more* sense, if you've seen another, previous bumper sticker. This is something like what happens when somebody comes along and adds a word or phrase to an existing bit of graffiti, thereby completely changing the original meaning, often with humorous results. A couple of examples of this brick wall editorializing (which humorist Jean Shepherd turned into very catchy book titles) are "Jesus Saves!" under which some wag had added the line "Moses Invests!" and the classic "In God We Trust! All Others Pay Cash!"

While visiting the Pine Tree State, you're apt to see bumper stickers, even official WELCOME TO MAINE road signs, bearing the state's most recent (and most boosterish) slogan "Maine . . . the way life should be!" If you venture north of Bangor, however (and I hope you do), you'll run across a variation on that theme. This one says: "Aroostook County, The Way Maine Used to Be." Ouch! Take that, you Swedish-car-loving, black-Lab-toting, soccer-and-mall-addicted "southern" poseurs!

Folks in "The County," viewed by many in the southern part of the state as the poor relations to the north, tend to think of Aroostook as the last bastion of pure, unadulterated Maine. Perhaps, making a virtue of necessity, County dwellers are apt to dismiss the more developed (and therefore more prosperous) southern Maine counties as being "just like Massachusetts" (a scathing invective indeed, when spoken by a native Mainer).

The "Aroostook County, The Way Maine Used to Be" bumper stickers, which began sprouting on pickup trucks and massive Buicks (the vehicles of choice in this large agricultural region) back in the mid-1990s, were the brainchild of Richard Rhoda of Houlton, a man with a seemingly bottomless well of enthusiasm for all things "County." After he came up with the slogan, Rhoda's wife had a few made up as a Christmas gift. These early examples, plastered on the family cars, generated a lot of interest and "Where can I get one?" comments.

Soon thereafter, Rhoda's son Daniel, a Houlton High School student with an entrepreneurial bent, went into business for himself selling the stickers. The rest is history. Before long you could buy them at almost any corner store in the north country. Even retail giant Wal-Mart had them flying off the shelf.

Sales of the bumper stickers peaked a couple years ago. But, you know what? That's OK. Better'n OK, actually. After all, every marketing fad runs its course sooner or later. The Rhodas had some fun with Aroostook pride, young Daniel gained some valuable business experience, and everybody got a chuckle. But, while folks in The County want to be successful, they know that it's important not to be *too* successful. God forbid that they ever end up accused by other Mainers of being "just like Massachusetts."

Tall Barney's Restaurant

Jonesport

When I asked John Lapinski, proprietor of Tall Barney's Restaurant, how he came to own the legendary Down East eatery, his response surprised me. "It was half your fault you know!" That got me hooked, and like Paul Harvey I just had to learn "the rest of the story."

Apparently Mr. Lapinski had been a longtime fan of my "Postcards from Maine" on *CBS Sunday Morning.* That's the "half" that's my fault. The other half of the blame belongs to National Public Radio. According to Mr. Lapinski, he hated his job in the insurance industry in his home state of New Jersey. "I was dying in New Jersey." He remarked, bluntly. "One day I was listening to a National Public Radio broadcast about the liar's table at Tall Barney's, and I called my wife from the car and said, 'We're going to Maine.'"

Come to Maine they did and within a matter of weeks John and his wife, Linda, were the proud owners of Tall Barney's Restaurant in Jonesport. The restaurant is located just on the mainland side of the Jonesport-Beal's Island Bridge. It's named after a legendary early settler "Tall Barney" Beal. The fact that Beal's Island is still populated by plenty of tough, no-nonsense folks named Beal makes it a lot easier to believe the "tall tales" that are part of the legend of Tall Barney Beal. John refers to Tall Barney as the Paul Bunyan of Down East Maine.

Tall tales and tasty treats follow the footsteps of a local legend.

Tall Barney Beal was, in fact, by all accounts a giant of a man standing over six-and-a-half-feet tall. But he was no bean-pole. His strength is as legendary as his height. Barney is frequently depicted striding along the streets of nineteenth-century Jonesport carrying a keg of flour on each shoulder. The locals like to tell of the time, during the Revolutionary War, when Tall Barney single handedly "whupped" a whole boatload of Canadian fishermen who had temerity to tell him that he couldn't fish in their waters.

"That's actually a true story." claims John, "That other one, the one about him punching a horse out and killin' him. I don't know about that one." "Hey John," I thought to myself, "why do you think they call it the liar's table"?

From my experience (my wife and I stopped for "suppah" on an evening in July), the restaurant seems to be booming. Fishermen still come in at the crack of dawn to gulp down a few cups of coffee and a plate of bacon and eggs before heading out to work. More often than not they make a return appearance later in the afternoon after a day of fishin' to prevaricate, exaggerate, and entertain. In the summertime they entertain the tourists. In the winter "When things are slow," as John puts it, they still tell stories, only this time they're entertaining each other.

When asked how the reality of running a restaurant in Maine compares to the dream he had when he moved up from New Jersey, John does not hesitate. "It's changed my life completely. I've got my sanity back." As to how the townsfolk in Jonesport have adapted to having "their" restaurant run by a couple of folks "from away," John claims things couldn't be better. "The people are just wonderful. They were skeptical when they heard that a couple of people from Jersey were coming up to buy the place. But I came up to be changed, not to change anything, and they accepted that quite well." Hearing that last line, I thought to myself, "Hey, this transplant from New Jersey just said a mouthful about life in small town Maine."

Steaming down the Road

Kingfield

For Americans raised on cheap gas and the gas-guzzling Detroit turnpike barges of the '50s, the OPEC oil embargo in the 1970s was a wake-up call. Long lines at the gas pumps got people wondering, perhaps for the first time, just how long all that cheap gas was going to last.

Today in the twenty-first century, $3.00-a-gallon pump prices at the corner garage have convinced more and more folks of the wisdom, possibly even the downright necessity, of finding an abundant, affordable alternative to fossil fuels to power our cars, trucks, and buses. But, which alternative? Full electric? Gas/electric hybrid? Hydrogen fuel cells? How about solar or biomass?

Well, for anyone interested in alternate automotive power sources, I can recommend a trip to Kingfield, Maine, and a visit to the Stanley Museum. If you're any sort of car buff, the Stanley name ought to ring a bell. The alliteratively named Stanley Steamer, a popular and powerful steam-powered car, was one of the brightest lights in the firmament of emerging automotive technology at the dawn of the last century.

I spoke with Sue Davis at the Stanley Museum, and she graciously agreed to fill me in on a few highlights of this American automotive icon. The Stanley Steamer was the most famous of the more than one hundred steam-powered vehicles produced in the early twentieth century. Once-popular brands like Locomobile and Prescott have long since faded into obscurity. The White Company, an outfit already well-known for its (non-steam-powered) sewing machines, also manufactured steam cars. Although they're no longer equipped with burners and boilers, White Freightliner trucks are still a common sight on American superhighways.

At the Stanley Museum you'll find lots of information on the golden age of steam cars as well as a good selection of Stanley automobiles, including models from 1905, 1909, 1910, and 1916. You can attend steam car workshops, and the proud owners of restored Stanleys have been known to travel from as far away as Australia to learn more about the brand and attend maintenance sessions.

In the early 1900s, of course, the notion of a steam car was a very natural one. After all, the sleek modern locomotives were steam-powered and steamships had recently eclipsed sailing vessels as the fastest and most commercially viable method of moving people and cargo around the world's lakes, rivers, and oceans. Even in a steam-driven century, however, the Stanley brothers' creation was a real star. In 1906 a Stanley Steamer set a land speed record of 127 miles per hour, making it the fastest production car in the world. It's a record that stood unbroken for the first decade of the modern automotive era.

OK, so steam cars are fast, and they zip around powered by nothing more exotic than good old environmentally friendly water vapor? Sounds like just what we're looking for here in the twenty-first century. Well, not exactly. According to Sue Davis, there are a few problems inherent in the design of steam cars. For one thing, they are extremely labor intensive. The driver is, in fact, directly responsible for a complex series of steps necessary to start the car and keep it running. You don't just jump in a steam car, turn the key, and drive off.

First, the driver must ignite the gasoline pilot lamp (something like the one on a gas stove). Thereafter, he or she is responsible for manually switching over to the kerosene burner (hmmm . . . sounds like an awful lot of fossil fuel to me), monitoring the burner, and controlling the amount of steam released to power the drive train. Sound complicated? Now imagine your teenage son or daughter doing all that while simultaneously eating a Big Mac, talking on a cell phone, and downloading MP3s into the stereo system. Um, I think maybe I'll just pick up a bus schedule.

Liston on the Canvas, Lewiston on the Map!

Lewiston

I was barely thirteen years old on February 25, 1964, when a young, brash, incredibly cocky twenty-two-year-old prizefighter from Louisville, Kentucky, named Cassius Clay confounded the oddsmakers and set the boxing world on its ear. He accomplished this feat by beating world champion Sonny Liston for the heavyweight title. My old friend and veteran TV reporter Bill Green of WSCH-TV in Portland told me that the fight, held in Miami, ended with a TKO for Clay in the seventh round when Liston failed to leave his corner. According to Bill, "Everybody wanted a rematch because few could believe it had happened, and *nobody* liked Clay!"

So how did the rematch for the heavyweight crown end up being held in Lewiston, Maine, of all places? "As I understand the story, they wanted to hold the fight in Madison Square Garden," says Bill, "There was some question as to what Liston's real age was. Liston was the kind of a guy . . . like Mike Tyson, that kind of a guy." Bill explained that the issue of Liston's indeterminate age meant that New York wouldn't approve the match. "Maine," he says, "would license Liston to fight."

Of course we would. Hey, this was big stuff for Lewiston. The new champion, now going by the name Muhammad Ali ("Though nobody would call him that," says Bill. "They *still* didn't like him!"), set up his training camp at the nearby Poland Spring House. Howard Cosell and lots of other nationally known celebrity sportscasters descended on the town. These included one man who would achieve that status later in life: Bryant Gumbel, then a freshman at Bates College, sold popcorn at the event.

There was a general exuberance statewide over the big event. According to Bill, the *Bangor Daily News* claimed to have "scooped the world" by announcing a day in advance of the fight that the bout would be refereed by "Jersey" Joe Walcott.

On the night of the fight, I stayed up pretty late and tuned in to the broadcast on my little portable AM radio. After sitting through what seemed like hours of undercard matches leading up to "The BIG EVENT! The World Heavyweight Boxing Championship, Live from Lewiston, Maine!," the big moment finally arrived. They'd even flown in a Big Broadway Star to sing the national anthem! They couldn't have made a better choice for the mostly Franco-American Lewiston crowd than matinee Idol Robert Goulet.

Well, looking back on it, maybe they *could* have picked a better singer . . . at least on that particular evening. I remember being perplexed that such a famous guy not only sang amazingly off-key but flat out forgot most of the lyrics to the national anthem. It came out something like "Oh say can you see? By da da da dumm dummm. . . ."

Unfortunately, it was a forgettable performance. But the fight itself has never been forgotten. At the opening bell, the heavyweights lunged out of their respective corners and began sizing one another up, a little poke here, a jab there. We all settled in for the promised slugfest. Then suddenly, two minutes and twenty seconds later, to be exact, the whole thing was over. Liston lay dazed on the canvas, with the young Ali taunting him to get up and fight. What? Was there a punch thrown? Did Liston take a dive? What the heck happened, anyway?

Bill Green tells me that the only person who actually *saw* the punch was Gov. John H. Reed. (Bill knows about this stuff. I made the mistake of betting against him one evening in a bar over thirty years ago, and I've never done *that* again.) According to the Gov, "That was a helluva punch Clay threw."

The rest, as they say, is history. The celebs left town. Goulet's voice and career survived the evening, and although folks might refer to him as "The Greatest!" *nobody* makes the mistake of calling Muhammad Ali Cassius Clay anymore.

The Sweet Waters of Bither Brook

Linneus

There aren't many Bithers in this world. A good proportion of them live in the state of Maine; of those, a good portion have roots or connections in Aroostook County. In the town of Linneus, there are a lot of Bithers. Unfortunately, most of them are in the town cemetery on the hill overlooking the fields and forests of this rural community.

All Bithers are related, in some way. There was one Bither (called Biter) who started the clan back in the 1700s. He lived in southern Maine. Some of his descendants moved to the wilderness of Aroostook County and set up homes and farms. My grandfather, Milton J. Bither, was born in 1878, and he lived for a time in Linneus with his many brothers and sisters. One of the Bithers married a cousin, also named Bither (well, the Roosevelts did the same thing!), but that was not in my lineage. My father, Donald Bither, spent his first twelve years on the family farm in Linneus, taking care of the sheep and the horses, chores that he hated. He went to the one-room schoolhouse until he graduated from eighth grade. Then he went into the big town of Houlton to attend Ricker Classical Institute as a boarding student.

People's names often are used to describe places, like Washington County. Even the town of Linneus has a nominal heritage—it's named for the Swedish botanist, Carolus Linnaeus. But not every family has its own river.

My family does. It's called Bither Brook.

Bither Brook runs between the Meduxnekeag River in New Limerick and Sawyer Pond in Linneus. The brook, not more than 6 feet wide at its greatest width, runs through the same woods and fields that my grandfather and father tramped around in long ago. When we were boys on a visit to the County, we cut down a sapling branch, baited our hooks with local worms, and caught little trout lurking in the same shady pools that *their* great-grandparents had hidden in.

A few years ago, my brothers and I took our father to visit the site of his old homestead, which had burned down and been abandoned many years ago. We made a stop at the spot where Bither Brook travels through a culvert under the road. My brothers and I took off our shoes and socks and dipped our toes in the cool water splashing over the rocks.

The Hindus make their pilgrimage to the Ganges; Western religions speak of crossing the Jordan. Here, in the backwoods of Aroostook County, is a shrine just as sacred, but only to those few people who carry the Bither name. To some people, it's just a little trickle of water. But to a Bither, the water in this brook flows in our veins, and washing our feet in it reminds us of who we are and where we came from.

The Moxie Man

Lisbon Falls

You've got moxie! That is, you *will* have Moxie by the time you leave the Moxie store in Lisbon Falls. At least, you will if the Moxie Man has anything to say about it, and believe me, he has plenty to say about it. The Moxie Man is Frank Annescetti, whose mission in life seems to involve proselytizing, evangelizing, and otherwise spreading the Gospel of Moxie to anyone who will lend an ear or an untutored palate.

What is Moxie? Well, in 2005 the Maine legislature declared Moxie the official state soft drink. But, in its heyday, back in the 1920s and '30s, any schoolchild could have answered that question. Back then (according to Frank, a virtual encyclopedia of Moxie trivia, legend, and lore), Moxie was the most popular soft drink in the nation. Swilled and ballyhooed by sports legends like Ted Williams and an impressive roster of big-name Hollywood stars, Moxie led all other soft drinks in sales, with Coca-Cola trailing a distant second.

Never heard of Moxie? Frank wants you!!!!

The original formula for the drink was concocted by a Maine man, and its name (Frank says it's most likely a variation of the name of a Maine Indian chief) added a new word to the American lexicon. According to the latest *American Heritage Dictionary, moxie* means "the ability to face difficulty with spirit and courage," also "aggressive energy and initiative." That second definition really hits home with me because as far as I'm concerned, just drinking the stuff takes a sizable dollop of "aggressive energy and initiative."

To put it bluntly, the stuff tastes awful. Oddly enough, the Moxie Man wouldn't necessarily disagree. He once described the experience of drinking Moxie this way: "You take your first sip, and it doesn't taste that good. Then you take another sip, and it still tastes kinda strong, bitter, like that. Then you take another sip . . ." The way Frank describes initiation into the Moxie Drinkers Club, you never actually get to *liking* the stuff. You more or less just *get used* to it.

But who cares what I think? To folks like Frank and the legions of Moxie fans who make the annual trek to Lisbon Falls for Moxie Day, the second Saturday in July (Moxie addicts from as far away as the British Isles gather for a sip of the sacred elixir), there's just nothing like the taste of Moxie. On that point we agree.

When pressed, Moxie drinkers often describe the taste as bitter. "It's not sweet," they point out, as if sweet soft drinks were solely responsible for the moral decline of Western democracies. Grasping for something the listener can identify with, they earnestly liken its pungent flavor to things like castor oil, horseradish, and bitter herb tea. Does that make you want to run right out and buy a six-pack? I didn't think so.

But buy it they do. The Moxie store has Moxie and Diet Moxie (I can only assume that it's even less sweet than the original Moxie, a terrifying thought) by the case and carton, as well as a massive array of T-shirts, sweatshirts, bumper stickers ("Moxie Makes Mainers Mighty!"), Frisbees, key chains, and the like, all in the distinctive orange-and-black colors of the original logo. Maybe there should be a bumper sticker that reads "It's Always Halloween When You Drink Moxie!"

Whatever else can be said about Moxie, it's clear that Moxie fans will go to great lengths to satisfy their exotic tastes. The Moxie Man is, of course, happy to help out. He does a brisk business filling orders from around the country and has shipped cases of the beverage to such distant locales as Taiwan and Moscow.

Sadly, though, even surrounded by a sea of Moxie, Frank Annescetti will never be completely satisfied. The Moxie Man finally, grudgingly, acknowledged that today's Moxie pales by comparison to the original. "I remember the original Moxie," he admits wistfully, "not this kid's stuff of today. Back then you would never open a bottle warm. You'd want the bottle ice cold. If not [he snaps his fingers loudly, in a dramatic imitation of the sound of an old-time Moxie bottle cap popping off] half of it's on your ceiling. The extra carbonation that was in it . . . the extra bitterness . . ." His voice trails off into a sigh.

What? Today's Moxie isn't as bitter as the original . . . as potent? Opening a bottle won't knock out a streetlamp 3 blocks away? No offense, Frank, but some of us would consider that a sign of progress.

Worumbo Mill

Lisbon Falls

The remaining buildings of the Worumbo Mill on the banks of the Androscoggin stand as a monument to the days when Lisbon Falls was the center of the universe, and to the lessons learned from a one-crop economy. Some of the buildings are from the late 1800s, and a major addition was made in 1920. Many of the buildings were lost in a fire in the early 1990s, but Worumbo still stands and is still operating.

In its heyday, in the first part of the twentieth century, the locally owned Worumbo Mill manufactured woolen products. Trainloads of fine wool from around the country would arrive at the mill to be dyed, spun, and woven into woolen blankets and woolen fabrics for clothing. Children of Middle Eastern nomadic tribes would gather camel hair, to be made into coats. Children of South American mountain villages would gather the hair of vicuña, which would be sent to Lisbon Falls, where it would be turned into an elegant, expensive, and trendy fabric. During the Eisenhower administration, a scandal erupted when it was discovered that a presidential adviser had accepted a gift of a vicuña coat. Fabrics made by the Worumbo Mill were recognized around the world for their high quality.

NEW HAMPSHIRE LIQUOR STORE ON THE CIRCLE

There are several out-of-state locations where you will meet a lot of Mainers. Some trailer parks in Florida are dotted with the cars of Maine snowbirds. The buses at Foxwoods casino in Connecticut carry more parishioners from Maine churches than show up at Sunday services. But one place you are guaranteed to encounter a substantial number of your fellow Maine residents is at a New Hampshire liquor store.

On a weekday in June, there were sixty-two cars in the parking lot of the Portsmouth liquor store, a number that presumably includes those belonging to the employees of the store. Nineteen of the vehicles had Maine plates. This number is easily enough to make a quorum for an AA meeting.

There used to be a discount liquor store in Kittery—if you could find it—that offered some competition for the Portsmouth facility. But government officials got tired of getting flak about the prices being lower for southern Mainers (who, as everyone knows, really could afford to pay full price). So, as for now, if you want to get cheap booze, you have to leave the state. You also have to be careful coming back in, because there are limits as to the amount of imported liquor you can transport in your vehicle.

New Hampshire, on the other hand, has a pragmatic approach to liquor. It wants your money. It probably hopes you buy the booze and go drink it in another state. So New Hampshire has easy-to-

Mainers stopping by the New Hampshire liquor store for a fresh fifty-five-gallon drum of coffee brandy.

locate stores, right off I–95. It has a big selection, good prices, and no sales taxes. And it has Mainers.

How can you tell who the Mainers are in the New Hampshire store? They're the ones that ask for the coffee brandy, Maine's official beverage. They probably won't go to the single-malt Scotch section. And whatever they buy, it's in bulk. A common phrase in Portland is "I've got to go to New Hampshire soon." They put their big boxes of booze in the trunks of their cars and head home. We're only hopeful that they wait until they get home before they start to sample their bargains.

The mill was the biggest employer in the village of Lisbon Falls, where the homes clustered on nearby hillsides housed some French Canadians, some Yankees, and many Slovaks, who contributed to the culture of the town (ask about the Upper Slovak Club and the Lower Slovak Club). There was a turkey at Christmas; there was a summer picnic and a baseball team; and the wages were, arguably, enough to live on. But the textile industry was unstable. In the late 1950s the owners of the mill sold out to J. P. Stevens Company, which closed the mill in the1960s and moved its textile operations down south.

A series of owners, with assistance from the town, tried, with only minimal success, to keep the mill going. Finally, Herman Miller, who owned other textile mills in the area, acquired the mill and its machinery. It was then that Worumbo came into its own. This worldwide center of spinning fine fabrics from many lands became the home of, you guessed it, polyester. The same looms that once wove fine vicuña coats for the powerful and well-to-do now warped and woofed their way into powder blue leisure suits donned at gatherings of mere common folk.

In addition to the mixed blends, the hundred-year-old looms now spin and weave cotton-based fabric. According to Allan Miller, Herman's nephew, the wool process adds a special texture to the cotton. The mill makes a variety of fabrics and products, including blankets sold in stores around the country.

In the Worumbo Mill Outlet store, you will see, in addition to the fabrics and products, spools and cogs from the old looms and an account book from the early 1900s. You will also see, along the walls of the store, large photographs of the men, women, and children proudly standing at their machines and asking, across the chasm of time, "What the hell is polyester?"

All Roads Lead from Rome to Lynchville

Lynchville

It's an icon of Maine kitsch, a picture of the sign that points the way to China, Paris, Norway, Peru, and other exotic lands, all, of course, located within the boundaries of our great state. The sign can have several meanings—one is that all the world's pleasures and needs are right outside our doorway. But do the towns have anything to do with their names? Heck, there isn't even a Chinese restaurant in China, though you can get french fries in South Paris.

Most Mainers who know the sign may have a distant memory of seeing it as a child, when in fact it was really just the picture. Does this sign really exist? Or is it like the guys they supposedly put on the moon when they were really in the desert?

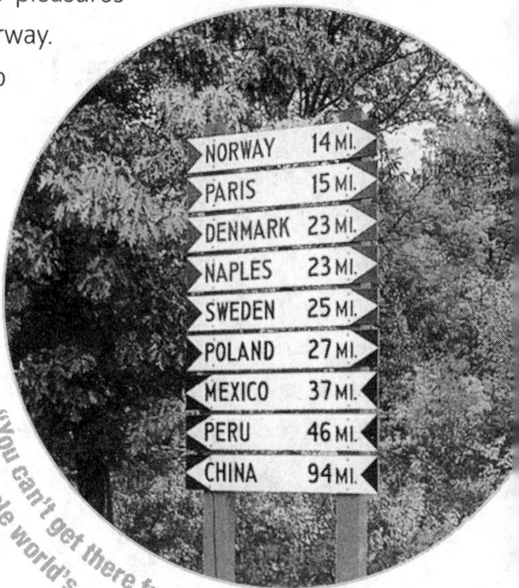

"You can't get there from here?" Why not? The whole world's practically in our backyard.

And if it does exist, how do you get there? I contacted John Stanley of the Maine Department of Transportation, and he had to look at the maps to find it. From Norway, you go to East Waterford, then head west to North Waterford, and you're almost there. Now, from West Paris, go to Bethel, then go south; where Routes 5 and 35 join together, keep on going. Of course, if you're coming from Sweden, you would take Route 5 north through Lovell, then head west toward East Stoneham. If you're coming from Berlin, which is in New Hampshire, you might as well be coming from Athens.

All of these roads meet up in the little village of Lynchville, where, at the convergence (or separation) of Routes 5 and 35, the world-weary sign stands. It's all well and good if you want to go to one of these places, but I still can't get to East Vassalboro. What's that, you say? It's right next to China? Ayuh, you could look it up.

We Breed 'Em, You Feed 'Em

Machias

Just like potholes, frost heaves, and ankle-deep mud, the arrival of the blackfly is a sure sign of spring in the state of Maine. Great clouds of the bloodthirsty critters cruise fields, farms, forests, and front porches looking for fresh victims. To fully appreciate the work of the Maine Blackfly Breeders Association, based in Machias, you should know a little bit about our local humor. The notion of discovering and awakening the laughter that lies dormant in life's difficulties (long winters, poor economy, death and taxes, etc.) is a central recurring theme in Maine humor.

This "when life hands you lemons, make lemonade" attitude is clearly the driving force behind the MBBA. How else are you going to explain the hundreds of bumper stickers in parking lots across the state proudly proclaiming "Save the Blackfly and Blackfly Breeders Association: We Breed 'Em, You Feed 'Em!" or the brisk sales of items like handmade miniature blackfly houses not much bigger than a postage stamp.

According to Holly Garner-Jackson, Marilyn Dowling, and Jim Wells, the current keepers of the MBBA flame, the whole thing began a few years back when writer Peter Crolius penned a series of tongue-in-cheek articles in support of the blackfly for local newspapers. In the aftermath of the writer's death a few years later, talented local sign painter and illustrator Marilyn Dowling promised the author's daughter that she and her friends would carry on the important work Peter had started.

And carry it on they did, in fine style. The MBBA won first prize in the Machias Fourth of July parade. As their float (a giant blackfly, of course) rolled by, volunteers ran into the crowd placing red stickers on bystanders' faces indicating that they'd been "bitten." Shortly thereafter, the MBBA sought and received official nonprofit status so that the loot from their big Fourth of July win ($1,000), along with proceeds from the sale of their growing line of blackfly products (my personal favorite being the snowstorm–style glass paperweight, which when shaken stirs up a cloud of tiny blackflies), would benefit local charities.

Where does the MBBA go from here? The sky (what you can see of it through the clouds of blackflies, that is) is the limit. You might want to check out their Web site, www.maineblackflybreeders.com for details. Good luck, and as we say up here in Maine, "May the swarm be with you."

Now That's What I Call Pie

Machias

Helen's Restaurant on Route 1 in Machias is a roadside oasis not to be missed. More than a landmark eatery, Helen's is a local institution. But just who exactly is this Helen anyway? When did she get started? And, perhaps most perplexing of all, how does Helen or anybody else get away with selling "world famous strawberry pie" in Machias, right smack dab in the epicenter of Maine's wild blueberry crop?

Let's start with Helen. According to the current owners, Gary and Judy Hanscom, the Helen in the restaurant's name was Helen Mugnai. Gary recalls that Helen's husband, Larry, opened the original restaurant back in 1950. "He started off with an ice cream parlor sort of thing," says Gary. "Then people wanted sandwiches and he did that. By about 1955 he was going full force as a restaurant. Then when the Navy people came and built the Cutler towers [an elaborate, cold-war-era early-warning radar array erected by the U.S. Navy in the nearby town of Cutler], that's when it really took off."

And it's been flying along nicely ever since. The Hanscoms have owned the restaurant since 1988, but Judy began working there back in the mid-seventies. I made my first visit to Helen's in the summer of 1970. Driving along the coastline of Washington County in late August of that year, folks kept handing me the same line wherever I went. "When you get to Machias," they said, "you've got to stop in at Helen's for a piece of that strawberry pie." Naturally, I stopped in.

This was, of course, the "old" Helen's, located on the Main Street of town perhaps a half mile or so south of the "new" Helen's established in 1983. Hey, distinctions like this are critical in small-town Maine. One thing I can tell you for sure is that the "old" Helen's certainly was *old*! Just walking in the door of the dilapidated wood-frame building, I instantly understood why the fishermen felt so comfortable takin' their supper at Helen's. The warped wooden floor of that old restaurant pitched and rolled almost as dramatically as the swells of the Atlantic Ocean just off the mouth of the Machias River. I recall that the food was hearty and plentiful and, as promised, the strawberry pie was fantastic. When I asked Gary how Helen's happened to get famous for making strawberry pie here in the heart of blueberry country, I was hoping for a long-winded colorful tale. What he said was, "No one really seems to know."

OK, so Gary didn't have a big story to tell me about strawberry pie. But, have you heard the one about Helen's *blueberry* pie? Here's Gary again: "We got written up in *Life* magazine last summer, and Helen's Restaurant has the best blueberry pie in the nation!" He continued, "The gentleman who wrote the article, Michael Sterns is his name, was in the restaurant four or five years ago. He was eatin' and critiquin' only we didn't know it 'til after he left."

I figured that since we were several minutes into the conversation before Gary got around to "best blueberry pie in the nation!" perhaps

Blueberry pie doesn't get better than this . . . anywhere.

there were a few more tidbits left to uncover. "So," I asked, "had any other interesting visitors lately?"

"Well, we always have a lot of truckers, of course. Then a couple of summers ago we had Martha Stewart in here." This sounded like a pretty good story, so I asked Gary how it happened that Martha Stewart made an appearance at Helen's Restaurant. "What happened was that she had taken her yacht out of Bar Harbor. She took it to Campobello and Lubec." Apparently at that point the yacht was fogged in, and Martha decided to return to Bar Harbor by land. "She was in her limousine, and she stopped at the restaurant one afternoon and settin' on the counter . . ." I happen to know that this figure of speech is actually Down East lingo meaning "settin' *at* the counter," but it conjures up an interesting picture just the same.

Gary and Judy Hanscom (and presumably a few of the truckers) had a nice visit with Ms. Stewart and her entourage. Over the course of the next hour or so she sampled several dishes and made arrangements for her "people" to contact them about filming a segment on blueberry pies at Helen's. According to Gary, there were numerous phone calls, but due to scheduling conflicts, "We couldn't get together on that

MIDNIGHT (OR NOON) AT THE OASIS AT IRVING MAINEWAY

They are everywhere along the highways of Maine, these oases for travelers. On a fog-shrouded night, the temple of Irving looms in the foreground, its structures and equipment bathed in welcoming light.

You might ask, what's so special about an Irving Maineway, a chain store that offers gas and sells cigarettes, coffee, and candy bars? A small number of Mainers will tell you what's so special.

You see, we are a frugal people; in fact, some folks might say we are cheap. We do not like to spend money on frivolities, and we do frequent places where our resources will be used wisely.

OK, but an Irving Maineway? The gas is the same price as elsewhere; the candy bars and beer are maybe higher than you would pay at a discount store. No, it's not that.

It's the hot dogs.

because of the end of the blueberry season. She might try again," he added philosophically. "We don't know." I'm with Gary. I don't know if Martha Stewart will be at Helen's again or not either. But I do know this: If you stop by Helen's, you can get a slice of the best blueberry pie in the nation. That alone ought to be worth the trip.

If you grumble about having to pay more than three bucks for a hamburger dinner at a place with arches, then you will feed yourself for less at Irving Maineway.

Near the back of the store, along a counter slightly littered with empty ketchup containers and paper scraps, located next to the coffee creamers and right above the trash container, you will find, side by side, two steam-type vessels, one containing packages with hot dog buns and one with steamed, red-snapper hot dogs. Taking care not to burn or scald yourself, you simply pull out two rolls, take out two of the dogs (that have been sitting there for quite a while, so you know they've been cooked properly), slather them with condiments (leaving the condiment packages on the counter), get a napkin, go up to the counter, and pay . . . $1.59.

That's right, Mr. Man, just a buck and a half for two tube steaks. The price has gone up about a quarter in the past three years, but it's still cheaper, and faster, than the arches. You fill yourself up until you reach home, or the next Irving Maineway. And your caravan heads off into the night, leaving the lights of the oasis glittering for the next cheap, hungry traveler.

Jamie Wyeth: Artist in a Box

Monhegan Island

Monhegan Island may well be the closest thing there is to a physical manifestation of the artist's muse. Generations of painters and photographers have made the pilgrimage to Monhegan and crisscrossed its granite and spruce contours seeking creative inspiration. The list of famous painters who have sought to capture the island's beauty includes such luminaries of American art as Rockwell Kent and Winslow Homer.

Of course, any list of famous American artists would be incomplete without Jamie Wyeth. Son of Andrew Wyeth and grandson of legendary illustrator N. C. Wyeth, Jamie is a brilliant painter in his own right. During a recent interview on the deck of his Monhegan home, Wyeth mentioned that he was only sixteen years old when he purchased the house from Rockwell Kent. When I exhibited my usual lack of tact and refinement by asking him where a sixteen-year-old would get that kind of cash, he said simply, "I sold a few of my paintings."

So the guy can paint, OK? But painting is a solitary endeavor, almost a form of meditation. So how, on an island crawling with tourists (not to mention other painters), does a man as famous as Wyeth manage to work with any degree of privacy? "Well," he said, "I paint in a box." Yup, you heard right, and according to Jamie Wyeth, it's a very effective tool. He stays out of the wind and weather, and most folks aren't quite snoopy enough to come up and peek in.

So, maybe I let the cat out of the bag (or the artist out of the box?) here, but, please, PLEASE, do me and Mr. Wyeth a favor. If you happen to find yourself traipsing around Monhegan Island someday and you notice a man making a painting in a box, DO NOT go over and bother the guy. Maybe you can just take a snapshot of the box or something. But let it go at that, all right? If ever there was an appropriate spot to paste one of those "Quiet: Genius at Work!" stickers, this would be it. Just let the man paint. Whatever masterpiece he's working on is likely to show up at a museum near you eventually, and when folks ask you if you've seen it yet, you can just flash 'em a mysterious Mona Lisa smile and say, "No. But I *have* seen the box it came in."

Zoe Zanidakis, Lobsterwoman?

Monhegan Island

I first met Zoe Zanidakis when she was hired by CBS News to ferry my producer, my camera crew, and me back to the mainland after a day spent on Monhegan Island discussing the history of painting on the island with Jamie Wyeth. It was clear from the moment we set foot on her awesomely shipshape 40-foot Young Brothers lobster boat, the *Equinox*, that, despite her gender and relative youth (mid-thirties), Zoe was unquestionably the captain of the vessel. We cast off and headed back to Boothbay Harbor, and over the thrum and roar of the powerful diesel engine I made the mistake of asking her if she was originally from "around here."

Call her a "pin-up girl" if you want. But don't say I never warned you.

ADIOS TO MADRID!

When is a town not a town? What makes a town anyway? These questions were raised—and perhaps answered—in 2000, when the remaining residents of the town of Madrid (pronounced MAD-rid) decided that they didn't want to have a town government anymore.

In its heyday the town, located on the Sandy River in Franklin County, had 500 residents. It was served by the narrow-gauge railroad out of Farmington and had employment for people in the wood industry, including wood product mills. But the years were not kind. Industry and people melted away. Taxes increased on those who remained. The post office, which had been in someone's house, closed up.

In 1999 the town voted, by a one-vote margin (of a three-quarter majority), to deorganize and to let the county and state governments take over its functions. The legislature approved the vote and accepted the town back into the state fold. As a result, local taxes were cut by about 50 percent, but local control over planning, roads, and education was lost. The state of Maine permits this trade-off, as it administers, with county governments, its "Unorganized Territory."

There were some hard feelings, according to an article in the *Portland Press Herald.* But town leaders tried to keep the community together by focusing on the past: At their final meeting, the town voted to give the Old Madrid School House to the newly formed Madrid Historical Society. The schoolhouse is on the National Register of Historic Places and is envisioned as a place to hold local functions. Any funds left over after the distribution of town assets went to the historical society.

And just like that, there was no town of Madrid anymore.

Joan Carroll, the president of the historical society, told me that the "town" is doing well five years after its demise. She estimates the population at around fifty. Residents who want a dog license or auto registration have to go to the big town of Phillips next door, but otherwise they don't seem to miss the expense and aggravation of having to operate a government.

As for the historical society, the Old Madrid School House isn't renovated yet. When it is, it will house memorabilia of the town that once was. Joan says the renovation may take some time, but there's no hurry. And why should there be? What's someone gonna do—complain to city hall?

The look she gave me was akin to the one Captain Ahab must have given Moby Dick just before he tossed the harpoon, and she informed me that she was, in fact, a "seventh-generation Monhegan Island fisherman." Smackdown on the high seas! I couldn't have felt more idiotic if I'd asked Wyeth the younger whether any other members of his family had ever dabbled at art. Since it's a long swim back to the mainland, I felt fortunate that years of toting city slickers around the wild North Atlantic have inured Zoe to bonehead remarks like mine. Otherwise, I'd probably be writing this from Davy Jones's locker.

Zoe first ventured onto the rolling deck of a lobster boat (her grandfather's) at the tender age of six months. The rest, as they say, is history—seven generations of it, no less. By the time she was in high school she'd already been working on the water for several years. She landed her first full-time job as a sternman while still in her teens and had her own boat, a 36-footer, at age twenty-two. She's been fishing ever since.

Like other Monhegan lobstermen, Zoe fishes "the season," from Trap Day on December 1 to Haul Out on May 29. When I asked her how many traps she tends, I felt stupid all over again. "The limit's 600," she said matter-of-factly, as if only an idiot would consider hauling even one trap fewer than the maximum allowed by law. In the off months Zoe makes a living as a certified scuba diver, running charter fishing trips or ferrying passengers to various destinations along the coast.

But lest you think that this bright, attractive, seafaring lady is all work and no play, she assures me that her credo has always been "If you work hard, you gotta play hard." When we last spoke a while back, she was doing a bit of playing, autographing her photo in the 2002 edition of the "Lobster Women of Maine" calendar. That's right, Cap'n Zoe (born on St. Patrick's Day) was Miss March. But don't get the wrong idea. She's fully clothed, standing confidently at the helm of the *Equinox*, looking every inch the hardworking lobsterwoman she is.

Lobsterwoman? Lobsterlady? Lobsterperson? Just what does one call a female lobsterman, anyway? "I'm a Monhegan Island lobsterman," she replies simply, obviously disdainful of lesser monikers, adding by way of explanation, "Go down to the island post office and ask the lady behind the counter how she likes being referred to as a 'postmistress.'" I politely declined Zoe's kind offer on the grounds that I'd already asked enough foolish questions for one day.

A New Life for Cumston Hall

Monmouth

Town halls in Maine are located in a variety of building types. Some are in trailers or modular buildings, some in abandoned schoolhouses, some in nondescript, functional brick-and-mortar buildings that have no character, and some in buildings that bespeak the importance of the governmental process going on within. But there is one former town hall that is a crown jewel of architecture. That is Cumston Hall, in the center of the small (population 3,350) town of Monmouth.

Cumston Hall. Not your ordinary New England town hall.

Cumston Hall, built in 1900, is a mix of architectural styles, from Romanesque towers and columns to Queen Anne–style textures. It seems too ornate, and yet too delicate, to serve as a public building. When it was constructed, it was ahead of its time because it boasted of indoor plumbing and electricity. It is listed on the National Register of Historic Places.

Cumston Hall is no longer the site for Monmouth's town hall. In the late 1990s, the town moved its operations to a more functional structure down the road. However, Cumston Hall still houses the town library.

In addition, 10,000 people visit Cumston Hall each summer to attend performances at the Theater at Monmouth, a professional theater company that performs Shakespearean fare in the hall's 250-seat theater, originally styled as an opera house. For several years in the 1950s, the theater was home to a Gilbert and Sullivan company. Gilbert and Sullivan operettas are still staged during the off-season. For more information on performances of the Theater at Monmouth, call (207) 933–9999.

The Monson Railroad: The World's Worst Little Rail Line

Monson

The Monson Railroad is one of the least illustrious rail lines in Maine transportation history. According to town history, the railroad was created in the 1880s because the Grand Trunk Railroad was laying out its tracks on a route that would bypass the town of Monson.

Perhaps to right an insult, or thinking that there might be a niche to fill, an entrepreneur set up a 6-mile, narrow-gauge road from Monson to Monson Junction. An additional 2 miles connected the road with the slate quarries. The little locomotive, called the "Peanut Roaster," never turned around. It just went forward 6 miles one way and backwards the other. The train, designed primarily to haul slate, also carried some passengers and some mail and freight. But not very well, and never at a profit. There's also the following poem, written by one H.D.:

The Monson Railroad used to run
Three or four trains a day for fun.
But their net profits the whole year through
Wouldn't buy the engineer one drink of home brew.
So after twenty years they changed their style
And now they only run a train once in a while.
Their timetable hangs there high on the wall
And looks like a blank sheet with a pencil scrawl.
Come over quite close or there's something you'll miss
And you'll find that the timetable reads something like this:
Train number one on track number two
Leaves Monson whenever they can find their crew,
If the weather is fair and the wind doesn't blow
They'll be back with the mail in a day or so.

Mercifully for all, the Monson Railroad folded in 1945.

Not Exactly Disney World

Mount Katahdin

Ask Mainers to name two of the most beautiful spots in the state and a typical reply will be (1) some place on the coast, and (2) Mount Katahdin. For visitors coming to Vacationland, the ocean is accessible. But the "greatest mountain"(as it's called) is remote and not designed for your average tourist. For those who love the mountain and its wilderness area, that is just fine.

When he visited Maine's backcountry in 1846, Henry David Thoreau wrote of seeing the mountain peak in the distance. His guide said it was

MANY BRIDGES TO CROSS

OK, so you have the outline of every state on the side of your Winnebago, meaning you've been there and done that in the lower forty-eight. And maybe you can boast, unlike most Mainers, that you have spent a night in each of Maine's sixteen counties. But here's a checklist for the day traveler, one that combines history, geography, and two centuries of bridge-building technology. The Maine Department of Transportation has compiled a list of bridges (not including pedestrian and railroad bridges) that cross the Kennebec River, from the Atlantic Ocean to Moosehead Lake. How many of these have you crossed? Can you identify the persons or places for whom the bridges are named? Here they are:

Location	**Name**
Bath–Woolwich	Carlton (old and newly reconstructed as Sagadahoc)
Richmond–Dresden	Maine Kennebec
Gardiner–Randolph	Gardiner Randolph (who was that guy, Gardiner Randolph, anyway?)
Augusta	Memorial (in memory of whom? I forget)
Augusta	Father John J. Curran
Augusta	Cushnoc Crossing (completed in 2005, it was originally called Third Bridge)

Location	Name
Waterville–Winslow	Donald V. Carter
Waterville–Winslow	Ticonic
Fairfield	Kennebec River East-Center-West
Fairfield	Clinton A. Clausen Bridges
Hinckley	George W. Hinckley
Skowhegan	Margaret Chase Smith Bridges
Norridgewock	Covered
Madison–Anson	Bicentennial Memorial
Embden–Solon	Embden-Solon (not the most original name for a bridge)
Bingham–Concord	Kennebec River
The Forks	The Forks
Sapling Township	East Outlet Bridge
Taunton–Raynham Academy Grant	West Outlet Bridge (I thought all of the outlets were in Freeport)

As we mentioned, this list does not include railroad bridges—these have their own history and charm—and pedestrian bridges. An example of the latter is the bridge between Winslow and Waterville used by thousands of mill workers who either couldn't afford or didn't need an automobile to get them where they had to go.

4 miles away, but it was "as I judged it, and as it proved, nearer fourteen." Later, in a footnote in *The Maine Woods* (1864), Thoreau named the very few white men who were known to have visited "Ktaadn" to date and added: "Besides these, very few, even among backwoodsmen and hunters, have ever climbed it, and it will be a long time before the tide of fashionable travel sets that way."

The moving story of how Percival Baxter acquired the land around the mountain and carefully deeded it to the people of Maine, along with a trust fund to care for it, is told in *Legacy of a Lifetime: The Story of Baxter State Park*, by Dr. John W. Hakola. A continuing theme in Baxter's stewardship was that of maintaining the wilderness nature of the park. The first gift of land in 1931, for example, contained the condition that the land "shall forever be left in the natural wild state, shall forever be kept as a sanctuary for wild beasts and birds, and that no roads or ways for motor vehicles shall hereafter be constructed thereon or therein." Subsequent grants of parcels of land were affected by pressure from neighboring Mainers and from landowners who had sold Baxter the property, so that "in the end, [Baxter] provided for land uses completely counter to his original wilderness concept."

Despite some changes in restrictions, Baxter State Park remains basically unspoiled. Unlike Yellowstone National Park or Acadia National Park, the park experience is not one of "getting away from it all by bringing it all with you." There are restrictions on vehicles—none over 9 feet high, 7 feet wide, or 22 feet long for a single vehicle or 44 feet combined. Only one vehicle is allowed per campsite. No airplanes, except on Matagamon and Webster Lakes. No radios, TVs, cell phones, chain saws, or generators. Gee, how's a family supposed to have fun?

Other modern recreational activities are also limited: No motorboats, except on a couple of lakes, and no snowmobiles, except on the Perimeter Road and on certain designated trails. The snowmobile trails are not groomed. Hunting is allowed only in a few townships; fishing is OK, but you have to have a license.

Perhaps the biggest surprise is that you can't bring your household pets. This was the same Percival Baxter who found the company of dogs preferable to that of humans. Many prospective campers have been turned away at the gates when the family dog is spied with his nose out the window.

It isn't only the regulations and lack of amenities that keep people away. Tom Chase is a former park ranger who now runs Katahdin Region Wilderness Guide Service in Patten, where he guides groups interested in hunting, fishing, and photography. ("I hunt there myself, to get away from people.") Tom says there used to be more people visiting the park (annual visitorship is now about 85,000), but gas prices have made the journey into the wilds more expensive. Other than folks who want more snowmobile trails, there isn't much pressure to open the park up. Even the prospect of a North Woods National Park in land bordering the park, as has been proposed, should not result in a change in the wilderness status of Baxter, Tom says.

Those who wanted to camp overnight at the park used to line up at the park office at the first of the year to gobble up spaces. Now, there are rules about advance reservations within four months of the desired date. See the park Web site for details (BaxterStateParkAuthority.com). Or see Tom Chase's site, www.katahdinoutdoors.com, for more park information. (Even the vicarious visits to Katahdin are breathtaking.)

For the more macabre-minded, there is a list of Baxter Park "fatalities," which details the heart attacks, falls, drownings, and airplane crashes that have claimed lives within park grounds, including the shooting of a local man by a "Canadian draft dodger" in 1944, followed the next day by the shooting of a Canadian draft dodger in a gun battle with authorities near Indian Carry Webster Stream. The outside world had intervened.

So, take your Winnebago to the seashore, but leave your dog and RV at home and take your backpack to Katahdin. While you're there, remember the words of Percy Baxter himself: "Man is born to die, his works are short-lived. Buildings crumble, monuments decay, wealth vanishes. But Katahdin in all its glory, forever shall remain the mountain of the People of Maine."

Golf o'er the Waves

North Haven

Every June for nearly four decades, a group of golfers has played in one of the most exclusive—and remote—golf tournaments of the Maine season. It's called the Gin & Tonic Tournament. Furthermore, it's exclusive because you have to be asked to play in the tournament by one of its members (all amateurs and all dedicated consumers of the eponymous beverage). And it's remote, because you have to take the ferry to North Haven Island and play at the North Haven Golf Club, a beautiful 9-hole course that skirts the Atlantic Ocean.

The North Haven Golf Club was designed in 1932 by Wayne Stiles, primarily for the wealthy summer residents of the island. This was the 1930s, before the days of the blue-collar golfer. Over the years, says Larry Beverage, who sits on the Board of Directors, there have been a few changes to the course. One of its feature holes is the 130-yard, par 3, sixth hole, which was redesigned to skirt along Waterman's Bay. "A lot of golf balls go into that bay," says Larry. There is one 500-yard, par 5, and several long par-4s, so it's "not a cow pasture-type of course." One time, before the days of the airstrip on the island, a Piper Cub landed on a fairway.

A few years ago, *Golf Digest* called the North Haven Golf Club one of the best 9-hole courses in the country. This was a mixed blessing for the 400-odd club members, who enjoyed the freedom from big crowds and the ease at getting a tee-time ("Basically, you just show up," says Larry). The impact of the article was not so great, however, as it is still easy to play a round without waiting. A day-tripper has to take the ferry over to the island and trek about a mile from the ferry terminal to the course (It's pretty easy to get a ride, according to most golfers). Greens fees are forty dollars all day, which means as many 9-hole rounds as you can squeeze in before the ferry comes to pick you up again.

The golf course is open from "as soon as it can open in the spring, until the fall weather makes it close." It is well-maintained by two full-time and one part-time employee. ("For a pro, we used to have some-one who was good with a lawnmower; now we actually have a golf pro.") And it doesn't appear that, despite its location overlooking the ocean, it will be converted to condos, "That's not gonna happen," says Larry.

The club sponsors its own tournaments, but the Gin & Tonic is the big event of the summer for a lot of New England guys. It was started by a guy who went from Colby College to be a teacher on the island (no, not the Great Imposter, that's another North Haven story). He invited some of his Colby fraternity brothers to the first tournament; they each asked some additional friends, and the event grew into a forty-player event, some of whom were island residents and the rest came from away for golf o'er the ways, and post-golf revelries.

No one wants to commit to the claim that it's the easternmost public course in the United States, but it certainly may be the farthest from the mainland. For the members and special guests, it's worth the effort to get there.

THE MAINE ACCENT

Very few aspects of Maine life are more consistently associated with the state than the famous (and infamously impossible to imitate) "Down East" accent. I suppose if anybody knows about this, I should. For more than a quarter century, I've been performing and recording in the Down East dialect and now, about three-dozen record albums, CDs, videos, books on tape,and a bajillion radio and TV ads later, I can state one thing with absolute certainty. In all those years, I have never, not even once, heard a truly credible Maine accent delivered by anyone who was not introduced to the dialect pretty much at birth.

Oh sure, you may run across some octogenarian who moved to Maine at the age of two months and thereafter never strayed more than a few dozen miles from, oh, let's say Stonington or Birch Harbor. Occasionally, you'll find a person like that in possession of a genuine dyed-in-the-wool Maine accent. But, unless you happen to fall into that slim demographic group, you're far better off to just sit back and listen. Feel free to enjoy the rich verbal patina, the mind-boggling inconsistencies of pronunciation, the hypnotic cadence and yogi-like breath control that are the hallmarks of true native Maine speech. But, unless you want to end up in the same leaky skiff with a whole bunch of "tried-it-and-failed" actors like Tom Bosley, Fred Gwynn, and Alan Alda, you'd best stay out of the actual conversation.

Here are a few examples of Maine speech that aren't likely to crop up anywhere other than the Pine Tree State:

ayuh (exclamation). Yes! *Don't even try this one. Here's a tip, though. If you hear someone pronounce it "eye-up," they're definitely "from away."*

doaw (exclamation). *No! The opposite of ayuh.*

cunnin' (adj). Cute. *This may be applied to inanimate objects, animals, and people. In Maine it would be entirely possible for a cunnin' girl to have a cunnin' puppy dog and live with him in a cunnin' trailer.*

spleeny (adj). Oversensitive, whiney, or person who complains too much. *"Ain't that kid some spleeny! He fell off the barn roof on Thursday and broke his ankle, and he's still whinin' about it two days later!"*

tilt, or **roto-tilt** (verb). To till the soil. *"It was so nice last weekend, I got out the Roto-tilter and tilted the whole five acres out behind that old DeSoto of Hubert's."*

In the decades since Roger Miller completely butchered the pronunciation of the city of Bangor, Maine, by referring to it as *banger* in his 1960s hit single "King of the Road," millions of people across the nation and the world have compounded the error. Please help stop the madness! Mainers refer to Bangor as either *BANG-or* or the slightly more old-fashioned version, *BAN-gore*.

Following are some other mispronounced place names along with their correct pronunciations:

Calais = *Callus*

Madrid = *MAD-rid*

Vienna = *Vye-enna*

Hooked on Worms

Orono

Imagine going fishin' and not having a worm. Well, I suppose you could use a tied fly, but there's nothing a trout likes better than a night crawler to nibble on while he's ignoring the hook underneath. Chances are, that crawler came from Taylor's Worms & Crawlers, an eighty-acre nature preserve in Orono.

Owner Dan Smith says there is nothing like a good Maine worm. "We ship Maine worms all over the country. People feed them to pets; they are good for digestion." Maine worms are better than those grown in the Ohio Valley, which has more clay. Ideal sizes for crawlers are "number 6 or number 7," corresponding to their length in inches.

Taylor's supplies stores and businesses (many of them convenience stores or mom-and-pop locations near popular fishing spots) with fresh bait year-round. It's big business, involving raising millions of worms on the preserve and importing specialty wrigglers from Ontario, Canada (Dan didn't mention if these worms say "eh?"). They ship worms in flats containing 500 night crawlers or 1,000 "dillies" (small night crawlers). Some of the worms are raised on local farms and dug by contracted seasonal diggers. They keep a three-acre worm bed of their own "in case of emergency" in supply from elsewhere.

Taylor's had grown some baitfish as well, but the aquaculture project is taking a rest for a while. The farm is host to many school groups who are part of the "hooked on fishing" project started by local sheriffs and game wardens. The kids get a kick out of going into the massive cooler and seeing the hundreds of thousands of crawlers. Taylor's supplies worms to the children to learn the fun of fishing.

Today's fisherman, says Dan, is not "an old guy with a pail and rubber boots." He's touchy and picky, and he's the only one who knows what is needed. He wants fresh, healthy bait. Taylor's times its production and its wholesale delivery to keep the product fresh (and you thought it was just bread deliveries that were time sensitive). The product is rotated every one to two weeks. It's all with both the fisherman and the store owner in mind. "Say you're getting up in the morning to go fishin'. You stop at Bubba's store to get your bait. If you get good product, you might buy something else at the store. If the product is bad, you're not gonna shop there anymore." Good bait, Dan says, is like a gas pump—it's something that brings the rest of the business into the store.

So, switch your bait today, and take a Maine worm out fishin'. The fish will like it, and so will you.

The Umbrella Cover Museum

Peaks Island

Many objects of everyday life have stories to tell. Just bring your imagination to any yard sale and you will find items with history—the chest of drawers with the bullet hole, the teapot with the chipped spout, the dog-eared paperback with illegible margin notes—if they could talk, we would hear a story. Maybe not an interesting story, but it would be a story.

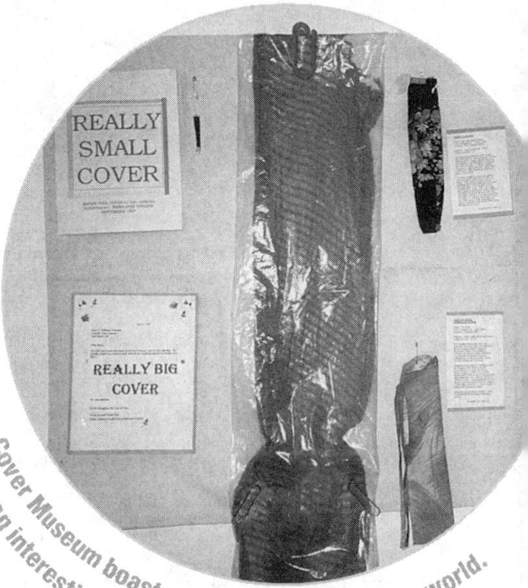

The Umbrella Cover Museum boasts covers from around the world. Here's an interesting place to spend a rainy day.

Nancy 3. Hoffman. Yep, that's her middle name.

And so it is with umbrella covers—the tube-like sleeves, sometimes called "sheaths" or "pockets," that keep umbrellas neat and tidy. According to Nancy 3. Hoffman, the proprietress of the Umbrella Cover Museum on Peaks Island, "Each cover has a story behind it." The Umbrella Cover Museum is dedicated to "the appreciation of the mundane in everyday life," says Hoffman, who runs the museum out of her home (visits by appointment only; 207–766–4496). Appreciation of umbrella covers is part of the appreciation of the wonder and beauty in the simplest of things.

Hoffman started collecting umbrella covers about six years ago, when some friends of hers couldn't bear to throw them out, "because they were too cute." A critical mass of covers developed, and now the museum boasts more than 300, including several new handmade covers, particularly admired for their symmetry.

The sheaths range in color and style from basic black to multi-patterned, and in materials from nylon to bullet-proof Kevlar. Hoffman bemoans the fact that umbrella manufacturers today either don't include covers or encase their products in clear plastic. "They've eliminated one of the last relics of tangible evidence of our civilized society," she says.

When she's not curating the mundane, Nancy 3. Hoffman plays accordion with the Maine Squeeze and with the Casco Bay Tummlers.

The Whales of August

Peaks Island

There is a cottage on the eastern side of Peaks Island that carries many stories. In fact, it carries a movie. *The Whales of August,* which came out in 1988, is based on characters and situations remembered and experienced by David Berry, who wrote the screenplay.

The title does not refer to Mainers at the beach or to the SUVs lining up at the Maine turnpike tollbooth on the last weekend before Labor Day. The movie is about the interactions of two elderly sisters—with each other, with friends and visitors, and mostly, with the island itself. It's hard to think of another movie where the location is such an important part of the overall work.

David Berry grew up in many parts of the country, including Philadelphia. But each summer in the 1950s and 1960s, he would come with his mother to stay with her two aunts, Jenny and Edith, in the cottage on Peaks Island. Aunt Edith had been a nurse. She was "an earth mother," says David, and became the character Sarah, played by Lillian Gish. Aunt Jenny was blind, with long white hair. Her character, Libby, was played by Bette Davis. The neighbor lady played by Ann Sothern was an amalgam of several island people, including a former society matron who had become something of a bag lady. The mysterious Russian Count, who made his home with several elderly island ladies, was as elegant in real life as when he was portrayed by Vincent Price.

The two main characters, real and fictional, lived as islands on the island. Other than working at the Trefethen Fair, Edith and Jenny lived in isolation. They spent hours looking out to sea (which the cottage faces). Some friends "from away" would come to visit and stay for a week, but the ladies were otherwise not sociable. In the 1950s, when the screenplay was set, the whales did make an appearance. Fin whales, some of them over 60 feet in length, would chase the schools of herring just off the shore. And everyone in the cottage would gather to watch from the porch, which hung directly over the water, giving the impression of being on the deck of an ocean liner. For other entertainment, there were games of cribbage, pinochle, canasta, and even a form of bingo played with darkened cards, so as to include the blind sister.

The cottage itself had been commandeered by the army in World War II to serve as a machine gun nest overlooking the submarine net in the channel between Peaks and Pumpkin Nob Islands. Soldiers lived year-round in this seasonal cottage, which had an outside privy and a well that required the occupants to break accumulated ice during the winter months.

In the twenty years after the war, during which David Berry was a summer visitor, the island was a different place than it is now. There were no numbers on the cottages to identify them by address. The roads had no curbs. There were five grocery stores (versus the one store now). There were no Realtors. But there was a community, shaped by island living. The community remains, even if the pace of life has picked up.

The house on Peaks was not used for the movie. Since there was no land in front of the cottage, it was impractical to photograph. The good news is that a cottage in Maine was not portrayed, as is often the case, by a site in Oregon, where, says David, "the setting sun will be in the wrong place." A big old cottage on nearby Cliff Island was used instead, and the cast and crew moved in for several months.

Lillian Gish was ninety-two years old at the time she played Sarah, and this was her last film. Vincent Price, Ann Sothern, and Bette Davis were in their late seventies; and Harry Carey Jr., who played the bumbling caretaker, was in his late sixties. The production company, Alive Films, was dubbed "just barely alive." David got the opportunity to meet with these legendary stars of stage and screen. "We won't see those stars again," he says. (Of course—those stars are all dead.)

We won't see that lifestyle again either. The cottage that served as the inspiration has just been placed on the market, taking it out of David Berry's family for the first time in eighty years. When Aunt Edith acquired the property in the late 1920s, Lillian Gish had left Hollywood and Bette Davis was on her way in. And in the water just off the porch on Peaks, the whales of August put on their own entertainment for the summer folks.

P.U. in Peru

Peru

It's not a roadside oddity, so much as a roadway occurrence. It's a combination of geography, the prevailing winds, and the nature of business and industry in the state of Maine.

When you're driving north on Route 108 from Auburn toward Rumford, you'll notice it, at first subtly, then unmistakably. In a car full of guys, someone might say, "Who cut the cheese?" In a family vehicle, the mother might inquire, "Has someone been indiscreet?" But everyone will notice it. It's the rotten egg, boiled cabbage smell of the paper mill in nearby Rumford as it wafts its way eastward and down the

Androscoggin Valley. The mill makes kraft paper, using a type of high-sulfur process that produces the odor. Some local people call it "the sweet smell of success"; others claim it is a warning of the presence of dangerous chemicals.

When we were kids, the first time we'd notice it was in the town of Peru, about 15 miles downriver but before you got to town. When we were kids, we used to say "P.U." when something smelled bad (I'm not sure what that stood for). So, even today, when I go through Peru—despite the Incan heritage, or the nice farms and houses—all I can think of is this: "Here we are in Peru. Peeeeeee yewwwwww."

Time and Temperature

Portland

The old clock tower in many a village center is a welcome sign. It serves as a landmark. It stands as an indication of the importance of commerce in our everyday lives. The classic lines of clock faces speak of tradition—they are, in a sense, timeless.

But the forces of modernization are constantly at work, acting as if change is always better than tradition. Leisure suits come to mind as a modern improvement over traditional vested men's suits. And so, the modern forces came to the time-telling function of the central city. Whether an improvement occurred is another matter.

The telephone company (back when there was just one telephone company) used to operate a digital-type time and temperature sign atop one of Portland's "skyscrapers" on Congress Street. Telling time digitally was all the rage. The sign was visible from many parts of the city, even in parts of the harbor. The sign wasn't as pretty as a clock, but it was there and it served its function.

When the phone company left, Maine Savings Bank moved in and added some words to the time and temperature sign, namely THE and BANK, which were flashed for several years. Some people going through Portland would look up several times just to see an indefinite article flashing on a sign. "What's with THE anyway?" The bank folded in the late 1980s, and the sign went dark.

The building's owner, who was not locally connected, wanted simply to get rid of the sign. Starting it back up for operation would have violated the state's billboard law. Suddenly, the new, improved, modern time teller became a cause for preservationists. According to local attorney Lee Urban, the sign was "an icon." Lee encouraged local fundraisers to kick in enough funds to get it started. The Chamber of Commerce managed the site, found advertisers, and added community messages (like SNOW BAN, to warn about parking during a snowstorm, and PLAY BALL, for the first day of Sea Dogs baseball). Lee convinced the legislature to amend the state's billboard law to get the sign flashing again. It took money to run. The lightbulbs, which look like pin dots from the street, are actually globes. Lee recalls going up to the sign on the top of the building and being concerned because the bulbs kept popping, which was expensive at $2.90 per bulb.

Today, the building is owned by the Libra Foundation, which was established by the wealthy philanthropist Betty Noyce. This organization has fixed up the sign. The building on which the sign flashes once housed a magnificent movie and vaudeville theater. It once had an indoor mall, called the Arcade, with shops and restaurants for the very urbane. Important people, lawyers and business types, had their offices in the Civic Arcade Building. But now the tail wags the dog. Everyone who does business in the building, when giving directions to the office, says, "We're in the Time and Temperature Building."

ITALIAN SANDWICHES ARE THE REAL MAINE FOOD

If you went into a store in the North End of Boston, or in Providence, Rhode Island, and said, "Gimme a couple of Italians, and easy on the oil," you probably would not survive the encounter. But in Maine, as in nowhere else in the world (including Italy), a request for an "Eyetalian" will get you an oversize hot dog–type roll, stuffed with ham or salami, American or provolone cheese, tomatoes, onions, pickles, green peppers, and black olives, liberally drenched with olive oil, and sprinkled with salt and "peppa." For less than four bucks, you can get a quick, cheap, filling meal that isn't too bad for you.

Italian sandwiches are the bread and butter of hundreds of mom-and-pop stores. Everyone has a favorite place, including the one that claims to have invented them, Amato's on India Street in Portland. My father used to walk a mile from his downtown Portland office to Mrs. DiBiase's store at the foot of Munjoy Hill to get her version, which was loaded with Greek olives. No real Mainer would be caught ordering whatever they serve up at a Subway store.

A few years back, the same type of advertising genius who came up with the "new Coke" and "new and improved Tide" came up with the idea of a new name for an upgrade—either "Real Italian" or "Italian-style," which defines an Italian sandwich, only more so.

Some of our favorite Italians are served at Terroni's (top) and Amato's (bottom) in Portland.

One of these items may have more Genoa salami and provolone cheese; but otherwise, it's pretty much the same, except it costs more. The upgraded Italian-style and Real Italian sandwiches have their place, but they raise this question: What were we eating before we had "real" Italians?

When people "from away" think of food from Maine, they almost always think of "lobsta." But it's a safe assumption to say that Mainers consume more Italians per day, day in and day out, than they do lobsters. An Italian, whether it's called "real" or not, is real Maine food. Maybe we should put one on our license plate.

Union Station Memories

Portland

Portlanders of a certain age have a shared memory involving a building. The Union Station, where the Maine Central and Boston & Maine Railroads met, had its own Gothic beauty. But it was what the station represented that made it more special. For many years, it was the gateway to the most important link between Maine and the rest of the United States. The shared memory involves a tragic time, in 1961, when the wrecking ball knocked the station, with its clock tower, into smithereens in order to make way for a distinctly ugly strip mall.

The real thing: Union Station in its 1920s heyday.

The destruction of this architectural treasure was the starting point for the historic preservation movement in Portland; it was also the catalyst for the formation of Greater Portland Landmarks. Some people felt that the wheels of progress made the demolition necessary and that, since the passenger-train business between Portland and points north and south was essentially gone, there was no need to preserve this drafty, somewhat dirty, and impractical building. Others wept real tears on that summer day and vowed never to set foot on the premises again.

The first big stores at the new strip mall were an Arlans, a low-budget department store, and a Big Buy, a low-budget, low-quality grocery store. Both businesses eventually failed, and new businesses have come and gone in the strip. Somewhere along the line, the owners named the mall "Union Station Plaza, trying to evoke the glory of the past. This name raises hackles to many a nostalgist—it's an insult, they say, to the glory days of rail life.

A poor substitute for the real thing.

The strip mall is still pretty ugly, compared with the castlelike structure of Union Station. But if you listen in between the sounds of traffic, shoppers, and music, and if you breathe the air, filtering out the smells of fried food and auto fumes, you might just discover a few of the memories that were made there over the eighty years of the life of Union Station.

> *"I sent two sons and a brother to war out of Union Station. Only one son came back."*
>
> *"I used to drive a seven-passenger Franklin taxi, and we drivers would get into some fierce fights for fares going downtown."*
>
> *"We used to take an afternoon train to North Station in Boston, see a Celtics game in Boston Garden, and take the late train home the same evening."*
>
> *"My grandfather used to work there. He rode a local train from Morrill's Corner over to Union Station, and at noon, he would take one back home for lunch and another one back to work for the rest of the afternoon."*
>
> *"My father and my uncles worked there as Red Caps [porters]. This was one of the few jobs available for black people in Portland in those days."*
>
> *"Elephants! One day the circus came to town. The train unloaded at the station and elephants pulled the wagons through Libbytown over to the circus grounds on Douglass Street. I will never forget that day."*
>
> *"I will never forget the day they tore that clock tower down. Part of me died that day."*

And there are other memories: The clock mechanism from the Union Station tower was rescued, despite its having been knocked over. It now stands in Congress Square. At many spots around town, homes are decorated with granite or wood salvaged from the rubble pile. There are probably more photos or drawings of Union Station in homes in southern Maine than there are of the iconic Portland Head Light.

After an absence of more than thirty years, train service to Boston was restored around the turn of this century. The Boston train now goes out of a new, antiseptic Amtrak station in Thompson's Point. It snakes its way along the Fore River on its way out of town, giving its passengers a distant view of the ugly backside of the building that took away the beauty—but not the memories—of days gone by.

Bowling Alone at the Woodfords Club

Portland

Not much has changed at the Woodfords Club since it was built in 1913. On Friday nights from October to April, men sit in the lobby, have a smoke, and talk about the weather and the news. At 6:30 P.M., they shuffle into the dining room, sing "My Country 'Tis of Thee," salute the flag, and sit down to their meal. Some of the members, on a rotating basis, wait on tables by bringing out platters of food. There's always whipped potatoes and yeasty rolls. Sometimes there's meat, sometimes fish. The men wear coats and ties. They eat with determination. They drink coffee, tea, milk, and water. At 7:00 on the dot, the president introduces the guests, then there is a report of who is in the hospital and who has died, and finally the program is introduced. It might be a musical group or a speaker with slides. If the program presenter has been properly informed, the program ends at 7:30, and the members retire to their evening's entertainment: cribbage in the cribbage room, bridge in the bridge room, pool or billiards in the beautiful pool hall on the second floor, or bowling in the five candlepin alleys in the basement. It's been this way for ninety years, and it is unlikely that it will change much.

Some things have changed. The price of dinner has gone from 25 cents in 1913 to $8.00 now—still a bargain. The pin boys who once worked in the bowling alleys were replaced by pin-setting machines, which click and clatter through their Rube Goldberg tasks. Though there aren't video games, there are computers in the basement on which you can develop your knowledge of this new technology. You can't smoke in the dining room, the card rooms, or the pool hall, as you used to do. Woodrow Wilson is no longer president, and women now have the right to vote.

Where things are as they ever will be.

The Woodfords Club was founded as a community organization for men in the Deering and Woodfords areas of Portland. Unlike the Portland Club and the Cumberland Club, it did not have a political (i.e., Republican) requirement. Social distinctions were not important—the railroad worker and the prominent attorney sat down to dinner together. No booze has ever been served, in part due to the club's proximity to a church, and in part because it seems to work out better that way. There is no secret handshake and no ritual requirements, though many members are also in Masonic or other fraternal organizations. If you are a member in good standing for forty years, you become a "life member," and your dues obligation (currently $150 per year) is waived. And, if you are a woman, you are not allowed to become a member.

The Women's Woodfords Club meets on Wednesdays from October to April. Its membership consists of wives, widows, mothers, daughters, sisters, and friends of male members. They have luncheons, fashion shows, a bridge club, and bowling, if they wish. Not much has changed for this club either. There doesn't appear to be any wish to "rock the boat" and mention the fact that Woodrow Wilson isn't president anymore and that women now have the right to vote. Each gender appears to enjoy its own club and its own way of running things.

In its heyday, after World War II and into the 1970s, the Woodfords Club had 500 members, with a waiting list of as much as six years. Families would use the club's pool room and bowling alleys on Saturdays. Bridge, cribbage, pool, and bowling leagues were full to capacity. As members grew older—and older—and started to die off, the waiting list for new members to replace them shrank (there is currently no waiting list). Younger fellows wanted to spend time with their families, including their wives, who worked outside the home during the week. Longtime members who were still living preferred the pleasures of Florida in the wintertime to those of Maine. A few new members trickle in each year, but their number is surpassed by the deaths and resignations of existing members.

The club shares a parking lot with the funeral home next door—rumors of an underground passageway from the club to the embalming room have not been confirmed. But this story is not about death. The Woodfords Club is an example of the decline in membership in community organizations discussed in Robert D. Putnam's book, *Bowling Alone: The Collapse and Revival of American Community*. Joining one group, Putnam found, will cut in half your odds of dying next year. Perhaps to keep the next-door neighbor at bay, the Woodfords Club may be the key to happy longevity.

Selling Hot Air Up North

Presque Isle

Aroostook County, Maine, is what some folks refer to as the "Other Maine." The notion of the "Other Maine" is itself a part of the Two Maines theory, which, although far from universally accepted, holds that there are actually two distinctly different "Maines." The first Maine is the prosperous southern tier. This would include about a 50-mile-wide coastal path running from Kittery to somewhere around Bar Harbor. This is the Maine that most tourists are familiar with and the area where most Mainers live and work. This is the picturesque "postcard" Maine.

The "Other Maine" if you accept the theory, is pretty much the whole rest of the state. This Maine is a vast area consisting of thousands of acres of forests, lakes, and streams; a wilderness where moose far outnumber registered voters and a hunting license is at least as important as a driver's license. Frankly, I've never been a "Two Maines" person. Maine is far too complex a place to be defined in such simplistic terms. Having said that, however, I must admit that Aroostook County certainly fits the "Other Maine" concept perfectly. What we mostly have up in Aroostook is lots and lots and lots of land; it's also really flat and, um, well, there are a few towns and plenty of potato fields and, um . . . did I mention that we've got lots and lots and lots of really flat fields up here in Aroostook?

Fortunately for the citizens of Presque Isle, sometimes what people who are planning a big historic event, like the first manned transatlantic balloon flight, really need is, um, well, a great big flat field would be good for starters. According to Allan Deeves, director of the Presque Isle Area Chamber of Commerce, a flat field was something the backers of the *Double Eagle II* expedition definitely needed for their transatlantic attempt. "There were other things, too, for topographical reasons. They needed to be in a place where they would be near the jet stream, where they could hit the jet stream and it would guide them where they need to go."

So it happened that on August 11, 1978, the world press assembled in a field in the Spragueville section of Presque Isle and watched as the *Double Eagle II,* carrying a crew of three, lifted off and soared into the blue Maine sky. They must have hit the jet stream right on schedule, because six days later the hot-air balloon landed safely in another field, this one in France, having completed the first-ever human-carrying balloon crossing of the Atlantic.

Soaring to new heights in "The County."

But it was not to be the last. Apparently, Aroostook really has "the right stuff" for this sort of aerial record-setting balloon adventure. A few years later, in 1984, and a few miles from Presque Isle in another field just south of Caribou another historic balloon flight took place. On September 18 of that year, carrying only pilot Col. Joe W. Kittinger, the *Rosie O'Grady* lifted off in Caribou and landed in Italy five days later. That flight set a new distance record, and the *Rosie O'Grady* became the first balloon to make a solo transatlantic crossing. Both the Presque Isle and Caribou launch sites now have historic markers and are open to the public, but the historic balloon flights left Aroostook County with more than parks and plaques to mark their achievements.

According to Allan Deeves, the success of these famous balloon flights showed the world that Aroostook County in late summer is just about the perfect place on the planet to fly hot-air balloons. "We have a hot-air balloon festival each year in Presque Isle the last weekend in August. We're going to have nine hot-air balloons next year," said Deeves, enthusiastically. "We had seven last year."

Hey, it makes perfect sense to me. After all, if you're going to take off in a big soft balloon and fly around sightseeing, you wouldn't want to take a chance on bumping into anything, right? Let's be honest here. Flying one of those things near skyscrapers and tall chimneys and so forth could easily make a person sort of nervous, don't you think? Yup, I say that for an adventure of that sort, you'd rather be safe than sorry. Why not lift off from a nice big flat field, for instance? And once aloft, perhaps you could fly across, hmmm, oh, I don't know, perhaps a few more nice big flat fields. Have I mentioned that we have lots and lots of nice big flat fields in Aroostook County, Maine?

THE BEST FLY-FISHING SPOT IN THE STATE OF MAINE

Now Everyone Knows the Secret

In the old days information about one's best fishing spots was top-secret. "I'd tell ya the best fishing place I know, but I'd have to shoot ya afterwards." Now, either because of the enhanced audience for fish bragging provided by the Internet or because the secret areas seem to get found anyway, there is at least a public discussion about such top-secret places.

A visit to Fly Fishing in Maine, www.flyfishinginmaine.com, not only offers information about top fishing spots but also records what was caught and what fly was used for the catch. The Webmaster, Dan Tarkinson of Portland, started the site a few years ago as a college project. Now it's a nonprofit organization that raises funds for conservation projects while sharing fishing information.

Etiquette dictates that you can take someone to your secret spot, but they aren't supposed to show it to someone else. Dan says some folks break the rule and post the location on the Web site. This information can be found among the latest spottings of the topless female fishing group, the Tacky Women Angling Team, and with information about "fly swaps." Armchair anglers can also learn of the potential dangers to native brook trout caused by the introduction of smallmouth bass in Rapid River.

Fly Fishing in Maine has a "conclave" in June, with a dinner, silent auction, and other events that raise funds for such conservation activities as the Rapid River Coalition and for such fishing-related activities as Trout Unlimited Youth Camp and Casting for Recovery, a retreat for women who have had breast cancer.

Dan's favorite method of fly fishing is catch 'n' release. "A lot of fishing areas are stocked based on the assumption that the fish will be taken. But this wouldn't be necessary if everyone threw 'em back."

So, what's Dan's favorite fishing spot? Besides the West Bank of the Penobscot, it's the Rapid River near Umbagog Lake and Pond-in-the-River. I'd tell you how to get there, but . . .

Sardine Man Welcomes You to Sardineland

Prospect Harbor

Sardine Man is distinguished from other Maine icons in several respects. First, he may be the only Maine giant to star in comic books (although Paul Bunyan might have snuck into a few). Second, he's the only big guy to start off in one location and end up in a new one just to avoid going to the dump.

Sardine Man is a 22-foot-tall, two-dimensional metal sculpture. He wears a yellow fisherman's outfit, including a rain hat, and carries the biggest can of sardines you'll ever see.

He originally stood at the entrance to the Maine turnpike, according to Charlie Stinson, the former owner of Stinson Canning Company. He was owned by the Maine Sardine Council. "The council had a lot of collective marketing activities, including setting up one brand of sardines that all of the packers sold," Charlie says. Part of their marketing activities included postcards and comic books featuring youngsters in Sardineland.

As times changed, so did the public taste, and by the early 1980s, the council thought Sardine Man had outlived his usefulness. Ever the Yankee, Charlie Stinson heard they were going to take Sardine Man to the dump. "I told 'em, if you pay to take it down, I'll go get my wrecker and take it away," he says. "I wasn't going to pay to take it down if they were going to do it anyway." So, off went Sardine Man to his present site at the entrance of Stinson Seafood in Prospect Harbor. The original man had two decorated sides, "but I set it up so it only needed painting on one side," Charlie recalls. He had the man repainted once in the ensuing years.

The factory workers loved having Sardine Man there. The sardine workers in the old days had a lot to be proud of besides having Sardine Man out front. Getting sardines to the public involved a lot of effort. In

Maine's Sardine Ambassador. The big man with the big can full of little fish.

the past, the fish were caught using stationary weirs, "when the fish come to you," says Charlie, instead of the purse-seining method used today, which has resulted in better catches but in overfishing. "We used to dry some of the fish outdoors in the sun," he says, instead of the more automated system used today.

One thing that hasn't changed is the hand packing. "You get good workers with the little fish, about eight or ten to a can, and they can make some money," according to Charlie. In its promotional material, the Stinson Seafood Company boasts: "Regardless of size or product, every single can is packed by hand—over 65 million cans a year! No machine has ever been invented that could match the speed, skill, and care of our Maine packers."

The smaller herring have been overfished nowadays. The packers concentrate on cut-up fish steaks, and the company imports some herring from other parts of the world for processing and repacking. Automated equipment does the nonpacking work at the Prospect Harbor plant.

Charlie Stinson sold his sardine business in 1992. The company, now called Stinson Seafood Company, has changed hands several times and has downsized its operations substantially. When I called the Portland office for information about the Sardine Man, the person in charge said he didn't know anything about the sign because he'd never been to Prospect Harbor.

If he did bother to go to Prospect Harbor, though, he'd find an industry that dates to the late 1800s, a plant that was started by Carl Stinson (Charlie's father) in the 1920s, and a 22-foot guy holding the world's biggest can of sardines welcoming him to Sardineland.

The Wilhelm Reich Museum: "The House That Orgasms Built"

Rangeley

Wilhelm Reich was either a "renowned physician/scientist" (according to the Web site of the Wilhelm Reich Museum) or someone whose ideas had "no status in the scientific community" (according to *The Skeptics Dictionary* by Robert Todd Carroll; SkepDic.com).

Reich, an Austrian psychologist who lived from 1897 to 1957, conducted many of his experiments in Rangeley, Maine. He believed that there was a form of energy that could be detected, measured, and harnessed. To capitalize on this energy, which he termed "orgone" in 1942, Reich created and sold orgone "accumulators" and orgone "shooters." These devices were banned in the 1950s by the Food and Drug Administration, which also burned some of Reich's books. Today, the Wilhelm Reich Museum in Rangeley features equipment used in his pioneering experiments as well as Reich's library, personal memorabilia, sculpture, and paintings.

What is this orgone stuff, anyway? It has something to do with orgasms. The "renowned scientist" described it as "the ability for total surrender to the involuntary contractions of the orgasm and the complete discharge of the excitation at the acme of the genital embrace," which creates an "orgastic potency." In many places, such talk would get the authorities steamed up. But in Rangeley, most people probably couldn't figure out what he meant.

Those who disagreed with Reich, and there were many, were called "orgastically impotent." So it was just as well that folks in the area focused on Reich's rooftop observatory, which provides a spectacular view of the surrounding area.

Reich attempted to demonstrate his "orgonoscope" to Albert Einstein, in Princeton, New Jersey, but when was the last time someone

TOP TEN STUPID QUESTIONS (AND TEN SNAPPY ANSWERS)

While we do enjoy and appreciate the many tourists who come to Maine, people "from away" have been known to ask some pretty foolish questions. Here are a few of our favorites, along with some snappy responses.

Q. Do the lobstermen always park their boats in the same direction?

A. *Sure, and every few hours they come back and park them in the other direction.*

Q. Does each lobsterman tend his own traps?

A. *Nope. The traps are all owned by "summer people." The lobstermen just go out and haul 'em in as a public service.*

Q. Can a person get a better price on lobster by dealing with the fisherman directly?

A. *Absolutely! Why don't you go down to the co-op this afternoon and ask for the manager? He'll tell you how it works.*

Q. (looking at live lobsters in a holding tank) Are they fresh?

A. *Yes, they tend to whistle and make crude comments whenever a pretty girl walks by.*

Q. Does this road go to Bangor?

A. *Nope. It stays right here.*

Q. How do you get to Portland from here?

A. *Generally, my brother-in-law takes me.*

Q. (from a tourist obviously loaded down with purchases made on vacation) Can we take this road all the way back to New York?

A. *You might as well. Looks like you've already taken about everything else.*

Q. Do you people always talk in that quaint dialect?

A. *Nope. After Labor Day we all switch to British accents.*

Q. Is it cold here in the winter?

A. *Of course not. People come here from Florida every January to get a tan.*

Q. You've been sitting on that porch for a long time. Don't you people work?

A. *Nope. Why do you think we call it Vacationland?*

from New Jersey listened to someone from Maine? One critic said that claimed results of the orgonoscope were suspect because Rangeley is so far north as to be affected by the aurora borealis, which in turn subjects the area to "high doses of cosmic rays." Maybe the presence of northern cosmic rays also explains why moose stand in the middle of the road at night.

Wilhelm Reich became a martyr to his ideas. He died in 1957, in Lewisburg Federal Penitentiary, where he was imprisoned for defying the FDA's ban on his products. His tomb, with its dramatic bronze bust, stands in a forest clearing near the museum. Some of Reich's ideas have not been fully released to the public, such as the "orgone-powered motor," which purportedly ran smoothly. This information is expected to be released sometime in this decade—just in time for the next energy crisis. Meantime, visitors to the museum can see the grounds, the guest cabins, and the scientific gizmos that go along with "the house that orgasms built."

The WGME Tall Tower

Raymond

Maine is home to a lot of big things—the Big Indians in Freeport and Skowhegan, the big Paul Bunyan in Bangor, the big lobster in Ellsworth. For a brief period of time, Maine was home to the tallest man-made structure in the world. This was during Maine's brief era of self-esteem, somewhere between the election of Clinton Clausen as governor and the Clay–Liston fight in Lewiston. Things were big. And so in 1959, the folks at the Guy Gannet Broadcasting Company built a television tower in Raymond that was 1,619 feet tall—taller than the Empire State Building, which was then recognized as the tallest building in the forty-eight states at 1,472 feet.

The tower was a monumental effort. Of course, its soaring height was surpassed in about six months by another TV tower somewhere. But it's still taller than the Empire State Building.

Today the engineers at the tower get to go up and down the elevator to the top, but they don't have to change the lightbulbs on the outside. Craig Clark, the chief engineer, says the tower may have been hit by lightning several times, but, thankfully, it's grounded. Some skydivers jumped off the platform a few years ago. Apparently, their chutes worked. Viewers of channel 13 news see the view taken from the camera on top of the tower, including storm patterns moving in over the lakes.

The tower has undergone some upgrading and renovation in the last couple of years. But it is still bigger—by far—than the Empire State Building. It also happens to be taller than the Eiffel Tower (a mere 984 feet) and the Washington Monument (just 555 feet). Not that we Mainers like to brag or anything.

Where Are the Snakes?

Raymond

Maine prides itself on not having several things that all of the other continental states have—a Red Lobster restaurant, for example (look it up!). And Maine does not have any poisonous snakes—or do we?

Rattlesnake Mountain in Raymond is not much of a mountain, but it does have a history of rattlers. The invaluable book *Historical Gems of Raymond and Casco,* by Ernest Knight, tells the story of Ben Smith, who, in the 1780s, traipsed up the mountain near his farm and found it "infested with the common or timber rattlesnake among the massive oak forest and craggy rocks." Smith named the hill after its denizens, and promptly began removing them. He caught the snakes, removed their fangs, and extracted snake oil lineament "as a cure for rheumatism and other ailments of the hard working settlers." Smith carried his snakes around as a sort of sideshow. He was bitten at least once, and he survived; however, he "acquired some of the characteristics of his friends as, according to surviving stories, his tongue habitually was darting in and out of his mouth."

Mr. Knight's tale of Ben Smith and Rattlesnake Mountain says that the snakes became extinct with the last recorded capture in 1870, their extinction due, in part, to forest clearing and forest fires.

The rattlers on Rattlesnake Mountain were not alone. Poisonous snakes in Maine became "extirpated," according to Philip de Maynadier, a wildlife biologist with the Maine Department of Inland Fisheries and Wildlife and the state's herpetologist. That word means that, although they are in existence elsewhere, poisonous snakes are extinct in Maine. We are located at the northern edge of the range of poisonous snakes, so the population was never great anyway. Then, human factors were superimposed—Phil calls it "persecution." There were published reports of rattlesnake bounties and rumors of a "roundup" on Rattlesnake Mountain long ago.

The mountain's namesake, the timber rattlesnake, is heavyset, with an average length of 3 to 4 feet and some growing to 6 feet. They aren't aggressive, says Phil, and won't bite except as a last resort. Their venom is not as toxic as other rattlers; few injuries and no deaths have been reported from timber rattlesnakes. They do use their venom to paralyze rodents, then they use their heat sensors to track the dead rodent, which they gobble up for sustenance.

Other Maine snakes of note are not poisonous. The black racer, a big critter, is on the endangered species list. The milk snake has a rattle, but it isn't poisonous; it just pretends to be (this author prefers not to verify that statement personally). The ribbon snake and the brown snake are listed as being of "special concern," as their habitat is increasingly being encroached upon by humans.

But, back to the first question: Are there any poisonous snakes, maybe some just hiding under a rock somewhere? Philip de Maynadier says that if there are any, they would most likely be in the western mountains (which does not include Raymond). Phil has not seen a Maine poisonous snake in person, but he has received reports from folks who claimed to have spotted them and are requesting protection for them. Phil calls these folks "underground herpetologists," but he appreciates getting their reports and tracking the information down. One of the sightings, as yet unconfirmed, was on Rattlesnake Mountain. Phil is concerned that there may be an effort to reintroduce rattlesnakes into Maine, perhaps to repatriate the serpents to their ancestral home.

The name Rattlesnake Mountain has survived, but other area features have changed their names, perhaps to avoid scaring settlers or summer campers. The two lakes that lie at the foot of the mountain, Great Rattlesnake Pond and Little Rattlesnake Pond, became Crescent Lake and Raymond Pond, respectively, leaving the mountain alone as a reminder of its now-extirpated denizens.

Think You've Seen "The Last Shaker"? Think Again

Sabbathday Lake

If you were among the millions of PBS viewers who tuned in to the Ken Burns documentary *The Last Shaker* a few years back, you can be excused for thinking that the Shakers, a small religious order who have made a big contribution to our modern American way of life, are an extinct breed. I'm pleased to report that nothing could be further from the truth. Far from being the spiritual equivalent of the passenger pigeon, you will find a half-dozen of these delightful folks alive and well and living in the Shaker community at Sabbathday Lake, in New Gloucester.

Here are a few things I learned while visiting the Shakers. First off, I had somehow formed the impression that Shakers were part of the austere, cranky, antitechnology religious crowd, sort of like the Amish in Pennsylvania. You know, dressing in black, driving buggies instead of cars, writing with charcoal on the back of shovels by candlelight, and so forth. No way!

The Shakers are, like, *way* into technology. As a matter of fact, they've been pretty much on the cutting edge of it since they first came to these shores from Manchester, England, back in 1774 and founded the Sabbathday Lake Community in 1783. In addition to designing and manufacturing the famous Shaker chairs and other furniture, the Shakers invented a lot of other cool stuff we use every day. The flat broom (as opposed to the round one the Wicked Witch of

The last Shaker? Not likely, bub! The Shakers are alive and well in Maine.

the West rode), the automatic washing machine, and even the dump truck are among the many inventions and innovations thought up by these pious, gentle, ingenious folks. By the way, in case you're thinking this is some kind of "get rich with God" type of religion, forget it: Shakers never bother to patent anything. When they build a better mousetrap, they just give it to the world, their way of saying, "Hey, God loves you!" Like I say, these are seriously nice folks.

Shakers also have a long-standing tradition of offering a free hot meal to any passing stranger in need of one. This has led to some interesting encounters. Back at the turn of the twentieth century, just such a vagrant, apparently an itinerant tramp, stopped by, enjoyed a bit of Shaker hospitality, and went on his way, fortified in body and spirit. It wasn't until a few weeks later, when a package containing a handwritten thank-you note and an expensive set of silver dinnerware arrived, that the stranger's identity was revealed. The anonymous "tramp" who came for dinner was none other than Louis Comfort Tiffany.

They also just love to belt out a tune. Shaker hymns are for the most part lively and upbeat, not unlike the folks who sing them. Their big hit "Simple Gifts," written by Elder Joseph Brackett right at the Sabbathday Lake Community, speaks volumes about their way of life. You know, it's the song that begins, "'Tis a gift to be simple . . ." Since Shakers take a pledge of celibacy, they must rely on converts to keep the community going. Fortunately, there are currently two new novitiates living with the community. I, for one, hope these newcomers decide to take the pledge and join up when the time comes. The way I see it, the world is a lot better place with a few Shakers in it. Let's all hope the last Shaker is many, many lifetimes away.

Bill O'Neil's "House of Rock 'n' Roll"

Saco

The sign out front is reminiscent of a '50s Wurlitzer jukebox, with artists like The Shirelles, Frankie Lymon and The Teenagers, and Fats Domino. But the real attraction at Bill O'Neil's House of Rock 'n' Roll is the man himself.

Genial and clean-cut, Bill lacks the surly swagger commonly associated with the rock world. Far more archivist than anarchist, Bill is passionate about the music and legacies of those who made it happen. "I finally got a couple copies of the first Five Satins 45s on the local New Haven label," he explains. "That was before they were on Ember, where they had their national success." Right, Bill, the Ember label. Heck, I knew that.

Bill opened his House of Rock 'n' Roll back in the late 1980s after an earlier career as a deejay: "I got fired at twenty-nine, and

Got questions? Just ask Maine's rock 'n' roll answer man.

when I was thirty-eight I asked myself, Do I want to get fired again when I'm forty-eight?" Obviously not. Although he's still on the air part-time, it's clear that Bill's "Heart and Soul" is in the House of Rock 'n' Roll. As Bill puts it, "Where else are you going to find all your Ultimate Spinach albums (now rereleased on CD)?" How about Moby Grape and Peanut Butter Conspiracy? Yup, right over there.

A big part of the fun here lies in picking Bill's brain. He is a virtual encyclopedia of rock trivia. Did you know that Harry Nilsson wrote the Three Dog Night hit "One (Is the Loneliest Number)"? Me neither. The more obscure the artist and label, the better he likes it. The very building we are standing in is in a way hallowed ground—it's where the '60s Maine rock band The Id (aka Euphoria's Id on another label) held their rehearsals. One of those 45s today is worth upward of $350. If you're interested in purchasing one, Bill would be happy to oblige.

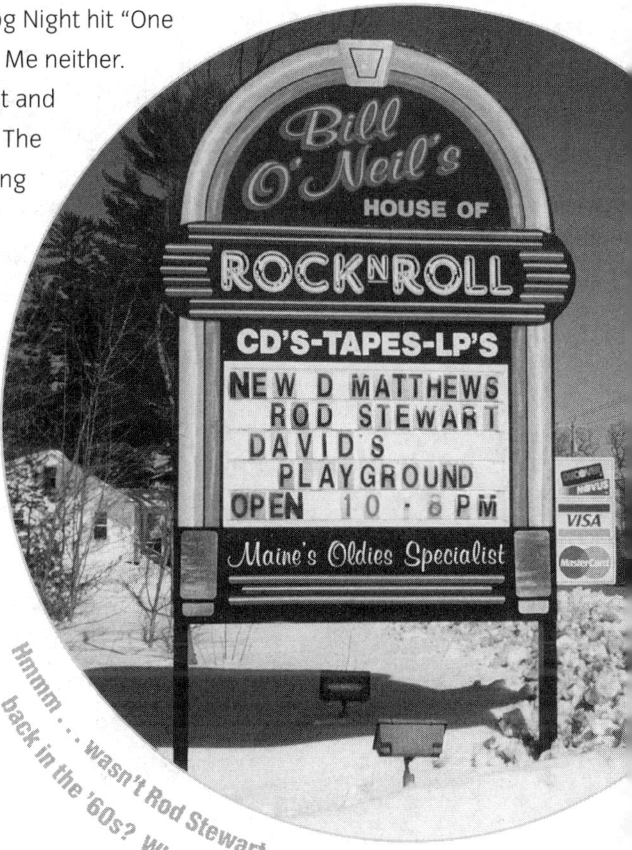

Hmmm . . . wasn't Rod Stewart with some Brit band back in the '60s? What was their big hit record?

Since I was there anyway, I figured Bill would be just the guy to help me solve a rock 'n' roll mystery that has been bugging me for years. In 1967 Sam & Dave had a big hit with the record "Soul Man." In the song Sam Moore touts his degree in "funkology" by belting out the line "I was educated at Woodstock." I always thought that was a cool lyric until I realized that the song came out two years *before* the famous music festival. So what was the "Soul Man" so hepped up about anyway? I asked Bill. I figured if anybody could clear up the mystery, he could. I figured wrong.

Bill dismissed the whole thing with a laugh. "You just *think* he's saying 'Woodstock,' " said Bill, as if numbskull questions like mine are the inevitable potholes in his daily commute. He went on to explain that some folks are convinced that the Creedence Clearwater song "Bad Moon Rising" includes the lyric "There's a bathroom on the right." Or that Jimi Hendrix pauses in the midst of "Purple Haze" to say, "Excuse me . . . while I kiss this guy." OK, I get the point, Bill. We're not studying the works of Shakespeare here. I must have forgotten: It's only rock 'n' roll.

Red Arrow Snowmobile Club

St. Agatha

It was 92 degrees in Portland in August when I logged onto the Web site for the town of St. Agatha and the Red Arrow Snowmobile Club. I knew right away it was in northern Maine because there was a note to "Click here for local snowmobiling conditions." The next screen had snowflakes coming down, and it reported that, as of March 29, groomer operators from Linneus to Allagash were still reporting excellent trail conditions.

I called Jim Raymond at R&R Snowmobile Repairs in St. Agatha. He works on two or three sleds in the summer months. He says in a typical year the snowmobile trails are good enough to travel on by Thanksgiving, and they are always in good shape through March. Usually there's enough snow to go out the first couple of weeks in April. That's a season of just under six months. The best sledding is in January, but people don't go out then because it's too cold. February brings the big crowds to the "top o' Maine."

The Red Arrow Snowmobile Club has some 140 members, which is a sizable number when you consider that the town of St. Agatha has only around 900 residents. If the city of Portland had a club with a proportionate membership, there would be about 10,000 members. The club is one of the central features of St. Agatha, as it's headquartered next to the town office and firehouse.

The Red Arrow Snowmobile Club takes care of 200 miles of trails, which in turn are connected to another 1,200 miles of snowmobile trails. That's almost the distance from St. Agatha to Portland.

Visitors planning to make a trip to St. Agatha in the winter should book accommodations at least two months in advance. If you are planning to go in the summer, you might have better luck.

When life hands you snow . . . drive snowmobiles!

Better yet, enter them in a race, like the Red Arrow Snowmobile Club's annual Snow Cross event.

The lovely town, originally called Lac A Menon due to its proximity to Long Lake, is also where you can find St. Agatha Historical House, the actual site of the home of Andre Pelletier. (I don't really know who he was.) The house and many properties along Long Lake were the subject of a fierce squatters' rights case in the late 1800s, in which the squatters actually won.

Besides bringing snow machines, snow gear, and legal history books, visitors might brush up on their St. John River "Valley" French. The town Web site wishes you *bienvenue.*

It also proclaims: "It is common to be greeted by strangers and passersby as you travel through St. Agatha as a welcoming gesture." Again, this is unlike Portland, with its own particular gestures for strangers.

To get to St. Agatha, take Route 162 from Madawaska through Frenchville. Or you can paddle up from Mud Lake to the end of Long Lake. Or, for about half the year, you can just get on your snowmobile anywhere in Aroostook County and follow the trails until you get to Snowmobile Route ITS–83, at the end of which you'll find a hot cup of coffee at the Red Arrow Snowmobile Club.

Robert Skoglund: Is He Humble? Just Ask Him!

St. George

How humble is the Humble Farmer? Well, you'll have to draw your own conclusions. Here's what I can tell you. The Humble Farmer, whose absolutely unaffected, natural Down East drawl has been drifting across the airwaves of Maine Public Radio for more than a quarter century now, is actually Robert Skoglund, humorist, after-dinner speaker, jazz musician, educator, radio host, and native of St. George.

I've know Bobby for about thirty years now, and I still haven't figured out the humble part. On the one hand, he has a penchant for self-promotion that would put even the most fanatical Amway salesman to shame. On the other hand, he is so dry and off-the-wall and his tongue is always so firmly planted in his cheek that it's hard to believe he ever takes himself or his career, or you or me or anything else, very seriously.

For example, the printed introduction Bobby provides for his after-dinner speaking work includes the following:

At present [Mr. Skoglund] employs 75,000 workers on his large farm. . . . They live in three hives.

Last fall, Humble spoke at a Democratic convention in Augusta—he was hired by Republicans.

We have two reasons for bringing Humble here tonight. One, we don't have much time, and he always forgets about half of what he has to say. Two, when we put this job out to bid, he was the only applicant who offered to pay us.

I first became aware of Humble (This is how he refers to himself. When answering the phone, his first utterance is always "Humble hee-ah!") back in the mid-1970s. I was just one of hundreds (well, perhaps dozens is more like it) of *Maine Times* readers who scoured the Personals each week. We weren't looking for a date, you understand. We were looking for one of Bobby's witty lonely hearts listings. When I called him and told him I wanted to put him in my book, he graciously agreed to supply me with about fifty pounds of promotional material (he just happened to have it lying around). Now, there's a really helpful, humble guy for you.

Among the treasures he sent me were these ads from days past. (Only a truly humble man saves his old personal ads from three decades back, right?) Here are some of my favorites:

July '77—Antiques dealer wants to meet attractive young woman interested in one nightstand.

December '78—Virile young man wants to meet attractive young woman willing to appear in Guinness Book of World Records.

Also December '78—Ornithologist wants to meet attractive young woman willing to sacrifice everything for a few cheep thrills.

November '79—Experienced traveler wants to meet attractive young woman who really enjoys being abroad.

Every now and then one of Bobby's personal ads drew fire for being a bit too risqué. I'm sure he picked up some flak for this one:

Lonely evangelist seeks attractive young woman eager to assume missionary position in Africa.

Even the progressive, liberal-minded *Maine Times* flat out refused to print this one:

Maine trapper seeks attractive lady taxidermist eager to mount four skins.

At this point, the single women among you will probably be relieved to learn that after fifty-four years as a confirmed bachelor, Bobby finally got hitched a few years back. According to Skoglund, he and his long-suffering wife, Marsha (whom he refers to fondly both on his radio show and in his monologues as "The Almost Perfect Woman"), have a very good marriage. You might wonder what charms Marsha employed to lure the Humble Farmer to the altar after so many years of confirmed (and judging from those ads, anyway, presumably very interesting) bachelorhood.

According to Bobby, it wasn't anything all that exotic: "I married her for her health insurance."

Goodall Park

Sanford

The national pastime is Maine's passion. Baseball is played in cow pastures (be careful sliding into third base!), in back fields, and behind schools, where fans sit in rickety bleachers outside in the fickle elements of weather. There is probably no more beautiful setting for the game than at Goodall Park in Sanford, a covered field with 786 individual seats and a history that few parks can match.

The park was originally built, in stages, in the early part of the twentieth century by workers at the Goodall Mills, the town's major employer. It was always a covered facility, but there originally were benches or bleachers for the fans. The stands were destroyed by fire in 1997; after receiving enormous community support, the new structure was completed in 1999, at a cost of $1.6 million. Blaine Jack, the park's unofficial historian, says the 786 new, individual seats were fit in the stands by making them an inch narrower than the standard 20-inch seats. There are also bench seats for 150 more. Dugouts are actually dug out, and there is a large press box on the third level. With night lighting, Goodall Park is ready for lots of baseball.

The park appears larger than its seating capacity. It's 419 feet to the flag pole in center field, 370 to left, and 295 to right, taking away the right-handed advantage provided by Fenway Park's Green Monster. The fences in the outfield do not have advertising, which provides a somewhat more pristine view of the action. And the field itself is immaculately maintained. Jack said that visiting coaches of collegiate teams have assumed that this was a minor-league professional park.

It's the history, though, that makes Goodall Park stand out. The semiprofessional teams of the early twentieth century battled it out here. One special day, the park etched its name forever in Maine baseball history. October 4, 1919, saw a record crowd watch the Sanford Professionals play the Boston Red Sox. As the headline in the *Sanford Tribune* said, the Sanford nine played "gilt-edged baseball," but the visitors

The seats are 1 inch narrower than the standard. Sit in these and you'll know if you put on a few pounds last winter.

prevailed on the strength of a three-run home run by Babe Ruth. The Bambino knocked the ball out of the park. The locals, though losers, were not disappointed: "It was a grand good game to watch," said the *Tribune,* "and many watched it—the biggest paid attendance of the season for the stores and mills were closed for the occasion." When Ruth made an error in the fourth inning, one fan remarked, "G'wan, you lout, get in there and play baseball. What d'yer spose I paid a quarter for your pictures for, anyway?"

All good things must pass. Despite Babe's ability in Sanford, the Red Sox traded him away, leaving the legendary "Curse of the Bambino" on both the Red Sox and their home, Fenway Park. The Goodall Mills closed in the 1950s, leaving just a name on its ballfield. The tragic fire at Goodall Park in 1997 destroyed the stands, old box scores, memorabilia, and a wooden statue of Babe Ruth. But today the curse has been broken, and Goodall Park is open for baseball once again, day and night, proud of its memories and looking forward to the next magic moment when a future star will knock the ball out of the park.

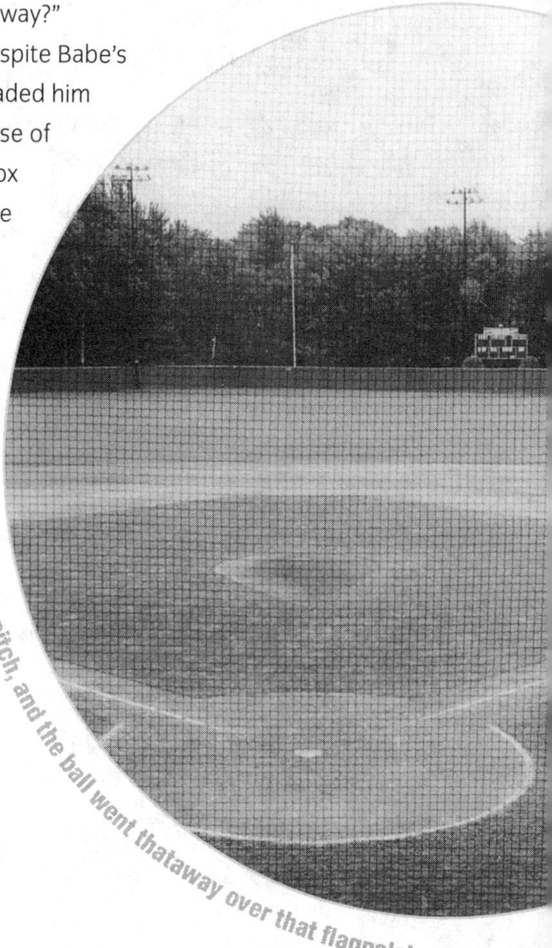

Babe hit the pitch, and the ball went thataway over that flagpole!

SOME THINGS WILL ALWAYS BE THE SAME

Everything in Maine is changing and evolving into a place just like the rest of the country. Maine will see more big-box stores, more TV anchors with blow-dried hair, and fewer locally owned businesses. There will be fewer "curiosities," no doubt. But there are some things that will remain the same about our state and about some of its traditions. We predict the following:

- We'll NEVER need a third lane on the turnpike to Lewiston, even though that city will be in a constant state of improvement.
- There will ALWAYS be work on the bridge between Brunswick and Topsham. The bridge spanning the Androscoggin at the waterfalls (sometimes called the Frank Wood Bridge) has been scraped, painted, repaved, shored up, repainted, and re-renovated for the past sixty years, and even if there is a new bridge, it will always be in need of some maintenance.
- The Red Sox will NEVER win another World Series. One time, when the stars aligned just so, will be all they ever get—it's back to "Wait till next year."

- No one from Maine will EVER be elected president of the United States. James G. Blaine, Ed Muskie, and Benjamin Bubar (he ran as a Prohibitionist) all tried and failed. Most of the rest of the people in the United States (especially in the South) don't even know that Maine is a state.

- People from northern and rural Maine will ALWAYS hate and resent Portland, even if it breaks off and floats away into the sea. ("It's just not part of the state," they will say.)

- Old Orchard Beach will ALWAYS be tacky, even if they put condos over the french fry stands. The town fathers try to clean up the image, but if the town didn't resemble a carnival, no one would go there.

- There will ALWAYS be a frost heave every spring on the Pleasant Hill Road, Brunswick, just after the Wilson place. I've lost a couple of mufflers on that bump, and my brother-in-law lost a whole transmission.

Babe's Store

Sanford

The magic day when Babe Ruth and the Red Sox came to Sanford in October 1919, the entire town turned out to greet the team. Marching bands escorted the Beantown Boys to Goodall Park, where the stands overflowed with fans who shouted with joy when Babe Ruth knocked a huge home run past the outfield fence.

The ball, it is said, went all the way out of the park and smacked into a small building in a nearby field. The building later became a store, and, because of its important place in local lore, it acquired the inevitable moniker, Babe's Store.

Whether it's true or not, the legend lives on.

Not true, says Lionel Perrault of Sanford. And he ought to know, since he owns the store. The building housing Babe's Store is located more than a football field away from the baseball park, which would make the Babe's homer longer than any in the record books. And the building wasn't even there when the ball was hit.

Most importantly, however, it was Lionel's father, Esdras Perrault, who started the store in 1941. Esdras, who was the youngest in his family, was always called "Babe." It was Babe Perrault who created his eponymous shop, selling sodas, beer, cigarettes, cat food, and little necessary items. Babe's son Lionel took over the business in the mid-1960s.

Of course, these facts have not bothered the mythmakers. Inside Babe's Store, you'll find a ball autographed by Babe Ruth's daughter, who came to town when Goodall Park was rededicated. And Lionel will tell you about how a high school student, doing a history project, had repeated the myth of Babe's Home Run being the basis for the store's name. Lionel told the student that this was not true. He then received a call from the girl's teacher, who told him to shut up and mind his own business. "They didn't want the truth to get in the way of a good story," Lionel says with a smile.

THE EXECUTION STATE?

Maine and Texas have some things in common: They border other countries, their people talk kinda funny, and they have a lot of NRA members. One thing they differ on, though, is the death penalty. Texas can boast of having a seemingly unquenchable thirst for executions, but Maine was the site of the first official execution.

It was in June 1790 that Thomas Bird, a sailor who had been convicted of the federal crimes of piracy and the murder of his captain, swung from the gallows in Portland. Bird had been a sailor on a slave ship off the coast of Africa. He had had an awful childhood, and his lawyers asked President George (Washington, that is) for mercy, but it was to no avail. A crowd of more than 3,000 (more than the entire population of the town) gathered at the execution site on Bramhall Square. The square was quite distant from the main part of town, but it afforded ample space for the crowd to watch the spectacle.

Bird admitted that he had lived a wicked life and had sinned mightily, but he denied actually killing the captain. It didn't matter. He was hanged, and the crowd was happy.

The hanging was the first to occur in the newly constituted United States of America. Texas wasn't even part of the country then. Of course, Maine was part of Massachusetts at the time, but we still get the credit. It was reported that pieces of the gallows were found more than a century later when the Maine Eye and Ear Infirmary was built. Now a marker at the Bramhall Fire Station commemorates the event.

Maine's taste for execution eventually soured. On November 21, 1885, Daniel Wilkinson was hanged at the state prison in Thomaston for the crime of killing a police officer. The newspaper reports of the hanging noted that the death was slow and gruesome. Perhaps if it had occurred in Texas, this would have been cause for joy among politicians. But the Maine legislature determined that there were other means of punishment, and the death penalty was abolished in 1887.

The death penalty had been questioned before in Maine after someone stepped forward to confess a crime for which another person had already been executed. This was in the days before DNA. The equivalent penalty in Maine today is a life sentence without parole. Some politicians are grumbling about the need to reinstate the death penalty for particular crimes, but their arguments aren't getting very far. We've been there, done that. If you want an execution, put on your Stetson and mosey on down to Texas.

Roger's Supa Dolla

Sanford

It's just a grocery store, but the name says a lot about how Mainers adapt to things. I imagine there was a guy named Roger. He wanted to have a 1950s-type "supermarket," where the "dollar" was king. Before he put up the sign, he tested the name on friends and family, using the spelling from the then forty-eight other states; but everyone pronounced it by dropping the "er." Why didn't Roger stick to the "proper" spelling? Probably because his name was Roger and he didn't want to put on airs. Or maybe, in true Yankee fashion, he knew that he could save on sign costs by eliminating a few letters. Another store that could consider the naming and cost factors is Rent-A-Center. After all, everyone in Maine calls it "Renta-Centa," so why not just adapt and make things easier?

This sign is missing a couple of ahhh's.

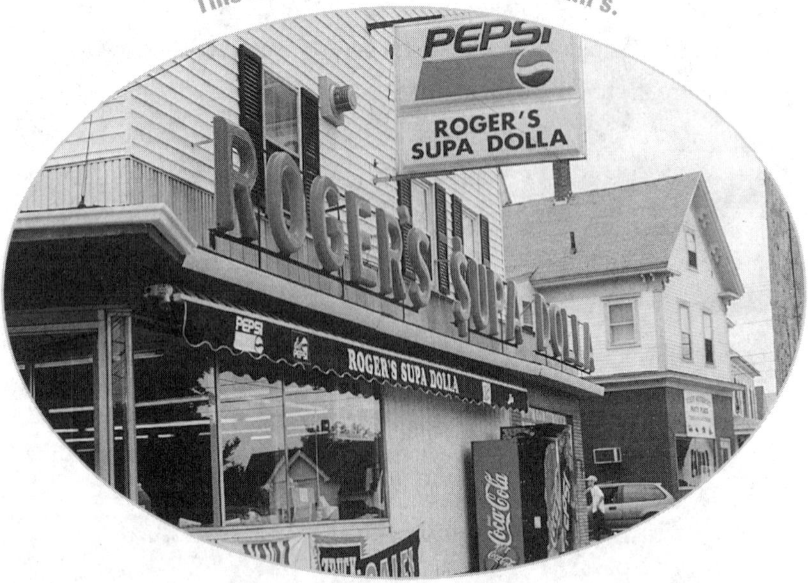

Meet Lenny, the Chocolate Moose

Scarborough

For reasons I've never fully understood, catching a glimpse of a moose seems to be at or near the top of a lot of folks' short list of things-to-do-while-we're-in-Maine. Although most natives are apt to have had this experience at least once and can give you suggestions about where and when to look, the likelihood of glimpsing one of these gentle giants in its native habitat is still a long shot.

Fortunately for those visitors with limited time and serious moose-gawking lust, there's always Lenny. Lenny is easy to find, mostly because he never moves. He's located inside the Len Libby Store on Route 1 in Scarborough. In the great tradition of roadside attractions everywhere, Lenny is grandly billed as "the world's largest chocolate moose." That assertion will likely go unchallenged if for no other reason than, as far as anybody can tell, Lenny is the world's *only* life-size chocolate moose sculpture. How big is life-size? Pretty darn big, it turns out—8 feet tall from the soles of his edible hooves to the tip of his chocoholic's fantasy antlers. Standing in a Maine woods diorama, Lenny looks for all the world like he's apt to turn around and walk out the back door.

Would you just hurry up and take the picture? My antlers are starting to melt!

Czechoslovakian sculptor Zdeno Mayercak and his assistants labored for a month to shape this startlingly lifelike quadruped from nearly a ton of pure first-quality Len Libby chocolate, the same handmade delicacy they've been turning out since 1926. I have to admit that when you factor in the beautifully painted Maine woods backdrop, the results are darn impressive. Visitors are encouraged to take snapshots, of course. Hey, come to think of it, if you can manage to snap one that's maybe just a tiny bit out of focus, you might actually convince the folks back home that you were standing 5 feet away from a real, honest-to-goodness Maine moose!

A store sign in Sanford. Since our worst problem is procrastination, we think we'll make that call later . . . much later!

Life in the Slow Lane

Scarborough

There are two kinds of bowling in Maine. There's "big ball," or tenpin, which you will find at a fancy spot with disco lights and automatic scorekeepers. Then there is "real," or candlepin, which is what goes on at the Big 20 Bowling Center in Scarborough.

Mainers of a certain age grew up thinking that candlepin was the only type of bowling, sort of like assuming that you would find Italian sandwiches and brown eggs everywhere. Candlepin bowling was even on TV, and it was a regular experience to go to the local alley for a birthday party.

The home of real bowling. No disco lights.

The original bowling pins actually were shaped like candlesticks, or dumbbells. In the 1850s the bigger, fatter tenpins were developed; because they were easier to hit, scores would go higher. Candlepin bowling was invented (or re-invented) in 1880, in Worcester, Massachusetts, by Justin P. White, who "thought that the game of tenpins was too easy." The pins are thinner than tenpins: 2$1\frac{5}{16}$ inches in the middle, tapering to $1\frac{3}{4}$ inches at the ends. The pins used to be wood, but thanks to an innovation started at the Big 20 in 1960, durable plastic pins are used. The balls are $4\frac{1}{2}$ inches in diameter, weighing from 2 pounds 5 ounces to 2 pounds 7 ounces, a lot more friendly for smaller (or older) hands than big bowling balls.

Although the scoring for candlepin is the same as for tenpin, the rules are slightly different. Candlepin bowling permits the use of "deadwood" that can be hit to knock down the remaining standing pins. And you get to use three balls to try to down the pins. In most candlepin centers, you keep score for yourself, with a wax pencil and a sheet of paper, not using some computer that supposedly knows how many pins you knocked down. You have to report your own score, and you have to do your own math.

No one anywhere has ever bowled a "perfect" game of 300. The highest score in Maine is 231, and the highest in an internationally sanctioned game is 245. Some folks think a "perfect" game of candlepin is when you get at least a 10 in each box—a theory that would get you laughed out of any big ball place, which is regularly adorned with banners for 300 strings.

The scores at Big 20 may not be as high as those in some other centers. Owner Chris Anton says that's because "we have honest lanes." Scores are impacted by several factors, including whether there is silicone on the plate that holds the pins and the height of the gutter. Even the pin-setting machines can come into play, as flying pins are knocked back into play after hitting the equipment.

Candlepin bowling's popularity is limited to Massachusetts, northern New England, and the Maritime Provinces of Canada. In the heyday of candlepins, downtown Portland had at least five bowling areas. It was pretty much the only bowling game in town, until it got nudged aside by the national popularity of tenpin, which happened at about the same time as malls began taking shoppers away from the locally owned downtown stores. Candlepin bloggers still bemoan the removal, despite its high ratings, of the *Candlepin Bowling* show from a Boston TV station in 1995; the station claimed it was not due to poor ratings, but that the audience was "not demographically attractive to advertisers."

The Big 20, also called the State O'Maine Bowling Center (both names came from a contest in the local newspaper), opened on Route 1 in Scarborough in 1950. Its owner, Sofokli "Mike" Anton, had owned a couple of bowling alleys in Biddeford. Mike had the foresight to know that people from Biddeford-Saco and Portland would get in their cars to come to Scarborough for bowling, rather than going downtown. The Big 20 offered twenty lanes for candlepin, tenpin, and fivepin (a popular Canadian game). Originally, the Big 20 hired pin boys brought in from Biddeford. They received about 3 cents per string, and they got a lot of splinters, which Mrs. Anton expertly and tenderly removed. With the advent of pin-setting equipment in the early 1950s, the Big 20 switched exclusively to candlepins.

There haven't been a lot of changes made to the Big 20 over the years. It still has the 1950s bowling pictures on the outside, though its interior decor has been upgraded from 1950s style to late 1970s. It's still a clean, family-oriented place, and kids still love the Big 20 for parties. They can lift the ball and roll it down the lane themselves, even if they have to use the bumper lanes that keep the balls out of the gutter.

Families crowd in on weekend afternoons. Ladies and older men have leagues during the day, and couples have mixed leagues on weekend and weeknights. There's a snack bar. Beer and wine are served, but that doesn't get in the way of the good family fun. The walls are adorned with photos and memorabilia, including records set by some Maine candlepin greats, like Dot Petty, whose 10-string total of 1,320 is very impressive. A string of bowling is a bargain at $2.90.

But, the biggest attraction of the Big 20 is its owner, Christo Anton, who is recognized everywhere as "Mister Candlepin." The son of Sofokli Anton and a great bowler himself, with a personal best of 189 and 460 triple (using wooden pins), Chris has appeared as a bowler and commentator on the local TV bowling shows. He cofounded the Candlepin Hall of Fame and served as chairman for thirty-five years. He's an ambassador for Candlepin bowling and talks enthusiastically about the loyalty of its participants: "There was a guy who just died last week at ninety-two. He was here on opening night in 1950, and he only missed two Tuesday nights since." Chris thinks that tenpin fans and candlepin bowlers are different crowds. Some people like to bowl tenpins because they get a higher score. But others like the challenge, and the more down-to-earth nature, of candlepins.

"The future of candlepin bowling," says Chris, "is up in the air." There are so many other things to do, including indoor sports and golf, that making a night out at the lanes not as compelling as it used to be. The number of leagues is down; other bowling centers are closing. But as long as there are avid fans of "real bowling," there will always be a Big 20.

(At Least) 76 Trombones

Scarborough

At eighty-one, Roger Snow of Scarborough is in the middle of a varied and busy musical career. Over a lifetime of music, he's played in, and led, all kinds of musical organizations, including a wicked Big Band that would put a gleam in the eye of Professor Harold Hill of *The Music Man.*

This is the seventh decade in which Roger has played professionally. While still a teenager growing up in Berwick in the 1930s, Roger played with groups at the Hampden Beach Casino in New Hampshire. The 1940s were the war years, and Roger served as an enlisted army musician, playing trombone and brass horns in field bands from Fort Devens, Massachusetts, to Presidio, California, including the Fort Lee BTU and Quartermaster Band (they burned a lot of energy in that one). He was commissioned an army music officer in 1949 and was a staff administrative conductor, serving through 1955. He played in several symphony orchestras, including those in Kansas City and Portland, from the 1950s through the 1970s. He played with the legendary Chandler's Band in Portland, the Jimmy Dorsey Orchestra, and Cal Cordeiro and his orchestra, and he led the Music Makers Big Band in the 1980s and 1990s.

Currently, Roger keeps active musically by playing with the State Street Traditional Jazz Band, with the Wicked Good Band (he's part of the Worms & Crawlers Orchestra component of the WGB), and by leading his own group, Jazz and More, which is a hit on the nursing home/assisted living circuit. He averages a couple of gigs a week.

For many of the years he was playing music, Roger was also a teacher and band director at several schools, finishing his career at South Portland High School from 1964 to 1983. He had many students who went on to careers in music themselves. Roger had a lot of wonderful musical experiences, but one of his favorites is preserved in a photograph in his home. There he is, on May 7, 1954, standing on a stepladder, arms upraised in front of a vast horde of musicians.

It was the Western Maine Music Festival, held at Pettingill Park in Auburn. Roger was there as host, in his capacity as band teacher at Webster Junior High School in Auburn. School bands from the western and southern parts of Maine had gathered for concerts, a parade, and a massed concert of all participating bands. By Roger's estimate, based on band strengths listed in the program, there were 2,350 young musicians in the crowd awaiting his downbeat. By any calculation, that exceeds the musical "76 trombones" section. There were fifty majorettes also, in short skirts, but in those days majorettes had to play an instrument as well as be marchers and baton-twirlers. Also in the crowd was Roger's brother, David James Snow, who played the French horn.

Making military music in World War II.

So, how was the music? "It was quite good," Roger says. "I saved a wire recording of the show for several years." How was the task of keeping all of those student musicians together? It went well, considering that not everyone had the same music for all of the pieces. Roger can still reel off the songs that were played that afternoon fifty years ago: "New Colonial March," by Maine's own R. B. Hall; Souza's "Stars and Stripes Forever" (this one had two arrangements with different numbers of bars); "Anchors Aweigh" ("We played a watered-down version," he said, not intending a pun); and the best one,

"The National Emblem March" ("It was better than the 'Military Escort,'" he recalls).

In the days of the massed band concert, Maine schools fielded large concert and marching bands. Roger's band at Webster Junior High had 150 members, including five sousaphones. In the next few decades, musical interest changed. Schools did not want to invest in fully instrumented bands, and kids lost interest in the marching band experience. (There is no indication that the decline of the band was because of a pool hall in River City.) At South Portland, Roger led a marching band that performed at football games, but it did not put on concerts—the acoustics in the old gym were pretty bad for band sound. Kids who played reed or brass instruments either found the guitar easier to learn or preferred to play in smaller jazz bands. Roger encouraged and led several school jazz bands, and he could get his groups to do a march or two. But we may not see—or hear—the big combined concert again any day soon.

The name Roger Snow is known to many as that of the composer of "Grand State of Maine," which is the official state song. But that is a different fellow, with a different story. That Roger Snow wrote a song that hardly anyone can remember. But this Roger Snow has made, and continues to make, music that no one can forget.

BAKED BEANS . . . IT TAKES SOME TIME

IIt wouldn't be a Saturday night in Maine without a bean supper somewhere. Look at the event listings for any town, and you'll find one at a church, a grange hall, or even at the town fair. Working on or at a bean supper is a form of old-fashioned community involvement. Attending a bean supper is a way to support the sponsoring organization, as well as a way to get an inexpensive meal with your neighbors along with the energy needed for a long winter's night. Even in the cosmopolitan Portland area, there are roving groups of friends who regularly meet at one bean supper or another every Saturday.

Now, we're not talking about dinners where the main attraction is roast beef, meatballs, veggie tofu, or just casserole potlucks. We are talking about beans. And it isn't a bean "dinner," it's a bean "suppah," if you please.

Where is the best bean supper? It's a matter of some discussion. Pownal, to the west of Freeport, claims to be "bean supper heaven" because it has several churches offering leguminous fare. The North Scarborough Grange, on Route 22, has several bean suppers throughout the month, sponsored by many different organizations. Some will claim that the best kind are "bean-hole beans"—cooked in a hole in the ground over hot coals—a method used at outdoor fairs and festivals.

A bean supper should have—in addition to beans, rolls, and coleslaw or salad—casseroles or macaroni-and-cheese dishes, coffee, and pie. Some bean suppers have ham or hot dogs or some other item from the meat group. The going rate as of press time is

CONTINUED

$6.00 for adults, $3.00 for kids, with special rates for families, but the price of everything is going up. It's still a bargain,though, and you will not leave the hall hungry.

The star of the bean supper is the baked bean. Various groups will guard their baked bean recipes more closely than the formula for Coca-Cola. But they all have one thing in common—they take time to cook. You can't just rustle up some beans from scratch in a half hour and call it good (except canned ones—see more later). It requires planning.

The beans (navy, pea, kidney, Jacob's cattle, etc.) need to be soaked for the whole night before the event. And then, with salt pork and other secret spices added, the beans need to be baked in the oven at about 300 degrees for at least seven hours. The cooker needs to check to make sure there is enough water after three hours and every couple of hours thereafter. The beans should be ready by midafternoon, just in time for the supper. They can be cooked in a clay bean pot, an electric crock pot, or a plain old metal sauce pan.

Using all of that energy and heat in the oven or Crock-Pot for seven or eight hours seems to conflict with Yankee values of thrift. In the old days, it was easy to put a pot of beans in the woodstove oven—the stove was working as a heating device for the farm kitchen. It seems that the best heat would involve cogeneration. In the obituary of Aldas "Douse" Carpentier, in the *Portland Press Herald* of October 14, 2005, his coworker at a wood products plant noted: "We had these big ovens that heated the acrylic and old Douse would bring in a pot of beans and cook them in it." As of yet, there have not been reports of giant baked beans cooked by the reactor at the nuclear power plant.

You can feed a whole bean supper with eight to ten pots of baked beans, depending on the size (of the bean, of the pot, and of the appetite of the diners). But what if you wanted to have thousands or tens of thousands savor this New England treat? You'd have to build a factory, like Messrs. Burnham and Morrill did on the edge of Back Cove in Portland. The factory was originally built in 1913 to manufacture B&M's big product, Fish Flakes, and to can Paris brand corn. By the 1920s, according to the company Web site, B&M began experimenting with making beans, "successfully resolving the high costs involved in the seven-hour baking process." The factory uses real brick ovens to maintain the heat. The popularity of factory-made brick oven–baked beans resulted in the doubling of the number of brick ovens, and eventually locating another factory on the West Coast. Today, runners on the Boulevard trail around Back Cove can get a whiff of the beans a-cookin', just like on a Saturday around the woodstove. For the home-made bean supper, B&M packs its baked bean products both in cans and in beautiful bean-pot–shaped glass jars.

If it weren't for baked beans, there would be less employment, fewer church activities, and less community spirit. There would also be the loss of humor, Maine-based and otherwise, resulting from "the inevitable consequence of consuming beans." However, as a good bean-iac will tell you, properly soaked and cooked baked beans don't produce even a whiff of gas—just enough energy to make it into Sunday morning.

Makin' a lot of beans at once, but bakin' 'em real slow.

Skowhegan Big Indian

Skowhegan

Maine folks like to talk about the importance of being a "native Mainer." The real natives, of course, would dispute the title if applied to someone whose ancestors didn't arrive in Maine until 1600. From that time until fairly recently, those who were here before 1600 were called Indians. Now, as a result of either political correctness or heightened sensitivity, the term Native Americans is used. For example, in Freeport, what was the FBI—the Freeport Big Indian—is now the MBNA—Maine's Big Native American. In Skowhegan, it's still the Indian, and it's a very big one.

The Skowhegan Indian, standing at the intersection of Routes 2 and 201, is 62 feet high and weighs 24,000 pounds. According to the Skowhegan Chamber of Commerce, the Indian was carefully crafted of locally grown white pine by sculptor Bernard Langlais of Cushing. To achieve a realistic likeness of local Indians, five Native-American models were used in the process of developing a face. It was a three-year process of planning and assembly, ending in the shipment of the Indian in two pieces to the town. Some longtime residents recall the day, in 1969, when the Indian arrived, lying on his back with his big feet up in the air.

The original intention of the sponsors of the Indian was to place him in a park, which would include a bandstand and other outdoor amenities. But the wheels of commerce churned differently, and gas stations and businesses surrounded the spot where he stands. Treetops partially obscure the top of the statue. According to Janeice Holmes, executive director of the Skowhegan Area Chamber of Commerce, a lot of people would like to see the Indian sited closer to, or right at, the Kennebec River, which would fit in with the theme of the Indian as hunter and fisherman (he's holding a spear and a weir net). Unfortunately, restoration experts believe that the monument would not survive a move.

Over the years the Indian has lost some of his color, due to natural aging. The Skowhegan chamber raised funds for restoration and preservation of him in 2002. It raised $20,000, which is being spent on testing for insects (those ants can be wicked trouble) and restoring the guy wires ("We don't want him to tip over," says Janeice). The restoration crew will try to match the original colors. More ambitious plans call for tree trimming, lighting, and a picnic area if possible. The chamber, and others with local pride, would like to make the Indian more visible: Janeice says, "The chamber office is 500 yards from the Indian, and people come in and ask where it is."

The town of Skowhegan, whose sports teams are called the Indians, is proud of its giant Indian. It draws people to the town, and it honors the Indians who lived in the area before European settlers and who made peaceful use of local resources.

The Skowhegan Indian was created with attention to detail and color. It is a work of "art," distinct perhaps from other roadside oddities. There are some people, however, for whom all "big art" is in the same category. For these folks the Skowhegan Indian takes its place along with Paul Bunyan and the Giant Walking Serviceman just as Andrew Wyeth paintings take their place among pictures of kids with big eyes and Elvis on velvet. While everyone agrees it's larger than life, the beholder will have to decide whether the Skowhegan Indian is art, culture, or cultch.

The Castle

South Freeport

The castle tower in South Freeport is all that remains of a legendary hotel that operated for a dozen years at the beginning of the last century. The Casco Castle was built by the owners of the electric trolley line to promote the line and to get city folks out to the seaside for a 50-cent shore dinner. The hotel had rooms for one hundred guests, spacious grounds, and a 300-foot suspension bridge over a ravine at its entrance. The castle was, at high tide, on its own island. It was a dream, and many old-time Mainers remembered the dream for decades after it was gone.

Fire destroyed the dream that was the Casco Castle. As the *Portland Press* reported on September 9, 1914, "At an early hour yesterday morning that famous summer hotel which because of its unique construction has attracted the attention of summer visitors from all over the country passed up in smoke, fire having razed the structure inside of a half hour." The *Press* went on to report that the proprietor had lost his clothing, a gold watch, and "a valuable bulldog."

The fire was so hot it burned the woodwork from the inside of the stone tower. But the fire did not destroy the tower itself, which gave Casco Castle its charm. The tower, based on a medieval design, remains. It was built of fieldstone, about 100 feet high. There was a staircase going easily to the top, and there were window slits in the sides of the tower, affording visitors views of the surrounding oceanside and countryside. Ships at sea

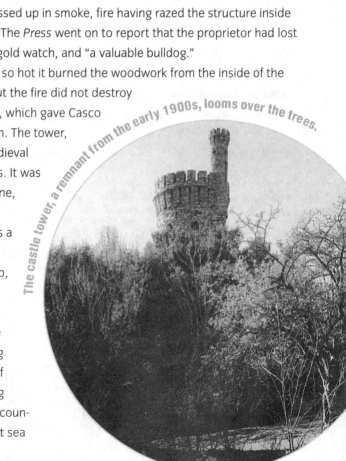

The castle tower, a remnant from the early 1900s, looms over the trees.

could see the lighted tower and use it as a landmark. (This was before the Big Freeport Indian, which can be seen from the British Isles.)

Trolley service continued to Freeport until 1929, but the tower was not a public attraction. Today, it is privately owned and not open to the public. The view of the castle from South Freeport isn't particularly good. However, you can get a good, unobstructed view of it from Winslow Park, which is the town park in South Freeport. Hikers in Wolfe's Neck State Park can also get a good look at it. Or if you're by the Haraseeket River, you can see what it looks like, and imagine what it looked like, from the water, with the moonlight drenching the gardens and lawns and the band playing "In the Good Old Summertime."

Fun with Tourists

Southport Island

His face has the authentic weather-beaten patina you'd expect to see on a man who has spent most of his ninety-plus years on or near the sea. The twinkle in his eyes and his wry grin are an open invitation to unsuspecting tourists. "Come on over," they seem to say. "Set right down. Go ahead . . . ask me a question." Not that Eliot Winslow will do or say anything untoward, mind you. He's not going to bite you or anything. It's just that after having spent several decades being asked the same questions over and over, Eliot's answers have been honed to a fine, dry, Down East edge. Asking Eliot one of the half-dozen questions a hundred folks before you have already asked is a bit like lobbing a softball over the plate to Babe Ruth. He'll hit it right out of the ballpark every time.

Eliot's career on the Maine waterfront in and around Boothbay Harbor is a colorful one that spans most of the last century. Among other things, Eliot's a real honest-to-gawd sea captain with the expertise to

Southport's secret weapon of maritime mirth.

confidently pilot vessels a good deal longer than the block you live on back home. Don't let the rumpled trousers, scuffed dock shoes, and khaki work shirt fool you. Eliot Winslow is a smart, powerful, and successful man. That tugboat with the big *W* on the stack tied up next to the lobster wharf where you stopped for lunch belongs to him. As a matter of fact, the wharf itself and the restaurant belong to him, too. You wouldn't know it to look at him, but Eliot has made, and well into his nineties continues to make, a very prosperous living for himself around these parts.

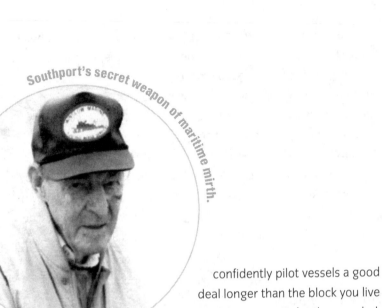

Never mind all that, though. To the average tourist who stops by Robinson's Wharf just across the Southport Bridge on Southport Island, Eliot's just another old geezer "numbin'" (his term) around the dock. If you're naive enough to buy that image, you've set yourself up for a good helping of "native wit" from a master of the genre. Eliot Winslow is actually a master storyteller who once appeared on Fred Allen's live national radio broadcast back in the 1940s. As recently as 2005, he was filmed live in concert at the Southport town hall. (The video of that benefit performance, entitled *An Evening with Eliot,* may be purchased from the Southport Memorial Library.)

By way of example, here's just one funny incident from Eliot's long career. A few summers back, Eliot was tidying up in front of the restaurant when he noticed a carload of confused tourists talking among themselves, pointing in various directions and waving a well-worn road map around. They drove off only to reappear and go through the same routine about a half hour later. According to Eliot, it took them the better part of an hour to make it back to the same spot for a third time, at which point they were ready for some native roadside assistance. Eliot, of course, was more than happy to oblige.

"Are you tryin' to get off Southport Island?" asked Eliot. They acknowledged that they were. "Are you tryin' to get off Southport Island by drivin' west?" Again they answered in the affirmative. "There's your trouble!" he said. "You can't get off Southport Island by drivin' west." He added helpfully, "If you do that, you'll be the first ones that've ever done it. If you want to get off this island," he advised, "you're going to have to go east, right back across the same bridge you drove across to get onto the island in the first place."

"But we didn't drive across a bridge," said the driver.

"You mean to tell me you didn't drive across no bridge to get onto Southport Island?" asked Eliot.

"That's right," said the tourist.

"Well, in that case," Eliot replied, "I take back what I said before. Your trouble is . . . you ain't here yet!"

Eliot swears this incident really happened, and, having grown up in Maine, I tend to believe him. But, true or not, it's a great story, and when you're talking to a real Maine geezer, that's pretty much the whole point.

Can a Funny Story Save a Life?

Stonington

Stonington, located on the southern tip of Deer Isle, is a picture-book example of a Maine fishing village. I once heard an old-timer remark, "Stonington was the last place on earth that God made. Then the Almighty went and decided to put saltwater around it so it wouldn't freeze up."

I can't comment on that, but I do know that, for better or worse, richer or poorer, in sickness and in health, folks in Stonington have been virtually married to the sea for many generations.

A few years back, in response to the tragic deaths at sea of two young island fishermen, Sue Oliver decided to start an organization. Along with other local women, mostly fishermen's wives (and daughters and sisters, too), she founded the nonprofit Island Fishermen's Wives Association. Of the organization, Sue says, "We try to raise funds for several different causes. If a fisherman dies or loses a boat, we try to help out the family." One of the first projects Sue and the other wives completed was a fishermen's memorial on the waterfront in Stonington. The hope was that when the fishermen passed the monument on their way to work on the open sea, they would be reminded to "be safe, have the right equipment on their boats, like that . . . do the right thing."

One of the most popular fund-raisers for the group in recent years has been the Fishermen's Wives Storytelling Contest. "We did it in January," says Sue, "so it was all local people." She added with a laugh, "No one comes here in January!" The event, held at the Island Center, was the result of Sue's attending a similar event at a waterfront bar in Boothbay Harbor, where she remembers the following:

"This woman got up, and she was telling a story about this guy who'd gone to Nova Scotia to pick up a boat. On his way back, he went below to take a nap, and he took his teeth out and left them to soak in a glass of water." According to the tale, the man's shipmates decided to play a practical joke on him by replacing the water with 90 proof rum. Sue continues, "Then they got worried that the rum would rot the dentures. But they figured 'Hey, the way he drinks, if they're not rotten by now, this won't hurt 'em any!' So when he got up in the morning, he took out the teeth, shook 'em a bit, put 'em in, and made a major face." Examining the glass, the sailor is said to have commented "It's a shame to waste good rum like that." Whereupon he added a bit of Coke and proceeded to drink his breakfast.

Although that story got a laugh out of Sue, she's dead serious about the work of her organization. "If we can save even one life, it will be more than worth it," she says. A recent Fishermen's Wives event may well have done just that. "We had the guys get in their survival suits, jump overboard, and swim to a raft. One guy got into his suit, jumped overboard, and discovered that it was full of holes. He almost drowned right in front of us all." After that embarrassing episode, Sue says that the chagrined sailor "got out of water, took off the suit, and threw it in the trash."

Perhaps that one incident, tragedy averted by a little good-spirited razzing, could serve as a kind of mission statement for the work of the Island Fishermen's Wives Association. What they seem to be saying is "A little laughter now can save a lot of tears later on."

The Prison Store: Shoplifters Will Be Prosecuted Immediately!

Thomaston

As any merchant in America will tell you, shoplifting is a major headache and a tremendous financial burden for businesses, particularly small operations such as gift shops. Interestingly enough, one of the busiest gift shops on the Maine coast, a modest storefront operation on Main Street in Thomaston, has no such problems. Despite the fact that many of the items on sale are small and easily pocketed by "light-fingered Louies," manager Joe Allen assures us that with a half million customers a year, pilferage is simply not a problem. He goes on to speculate that perhaps the uniformed guards patrolling the aisles may have something to do with it. Then again, it's very possible that the sales staff, a half dozen or so inmates from the Maine State Prison, create a certain "crime doesn't pay" ambience.

When it opened, the store was conveniently located right next door to the prison. But times change. All the original prison buildings were razed back in the spring of 2002, and the inmates were relocated to a new facility in Warren. But, the store—and its staff—stayed behind on tourist-friendly coastal Route 1. Hey, you have a problem with that? I suggest you take it up with the warden.

Need a sign? No problem, Warden.

The Maine State Prison Showroom, commonly referred to as the "prison store," has been doing a brisk business in downtown Thomaston since the Great Depression. The merchandise consists of high-quality furniture and handcrafted novelty items built by inmates in the prison workshop. They're not working for 10 cents an hour, either. The inmates in the program design their own projects and essentially run a small manufacturing business behind bars. Each inmate is allowed by law to earn a maximum of $10,000 per year (gross). Proceeds from their work often go to make restitution to victims of their crimes or to help support their families on the outside.

There is something a little strange about buying items made and sold by prisoners. A lot of folks notice that the original crafts projects tend to have an ironic twist. For example, the name of the wooden schooner model for sale in the showroom window, *Freedom's Way,* makes it hard to forget exactly where and by whom the vessel was built. Parking for the prison store is located out back. To keep you from blocking the loading ramp, the prisoners made a sign reading Loading Zone. Parked Vehicles Will Be Towed. How can you tell that the sign was made by prisoners? Each word is printed on its own individual license plate! Hey, at least they aren't doing time in New Hampshire, where all the plates stamped out by the inmates read Live Free or Die.

I've Been Meaning to Stop By Moody's Diner

Waldoboro

If you randomly stopped fifty Mainers on the street and asked whether they'd ever been to Moody's Diner on coastal Route 1 in Waldoboro, most likely forty-eight of them would say they had and the other two would say they'd been meaning to, but there's always a long line of folks waiting to get in. What is it that makes Moody's such a Maine land-

When you start out with a good idea . . .

mark, anyway? When I called to pose that very question to owner/manager Nancy Moody Genthner, granddaughter of Percy Moody, who founded the wildly popular eatery back in the 1920s, I was told that she would be happy to discuss the matter, but it might be several hours before she could call me back. It seems there's quite a line right now and she's kinda busy. Big surprise.

Meanwhile, here's what I already know. Stepping in the front door at Moody's Diner (once you've made it through that almost inevitable waiting line) is like stepping back in time. Moody's isn't a nostalgic remake of anything. Moody's Diner is the culinary arts version of the old line "If it ain't broke, don't fix it." You see that ancient faded linoleum countertop? The one with the ruts worn in it from generations of customers sliding the salt, pepper, sugar, and ketchup back and forth twenty-four hours a day? That's Moody's Diner! How about the waitress who can probably recall the day she served President Taft a third slice of pie and can definitely reel off a list of about forty homemade desserts in a tenth of the time it takes you to decide? That's Moody's Diner!

And if you're thinking you'll beat the rush and stop by late at night when things are slow, better think again. That trademark orange-and-green hand-lettered Moody's sign with the neon trim is, to the weary traveler, what a porch light is to a moth. Ayuh, Moody's just plain draws 'em in. But, by all means, if you get the chance, stop by. It'll be an experience you won't soon forget. Once you've scarfed down a hot open-faced pork sandwich topped off with a cup of coffee and a slice of homemade pie, you too will be telling all your friends that you've eaten at Moody's Diner. And when they say "I've been meaning to do that, but every time I drive by the place is packed," at least you'll finally know why.

. . . folks will beat a path to your door.

TRANSPORTATION TRIVIA

Did you know . . .?

1. Shortest numbered highway route in Maine: Route 217 in Phippsburg from Route 209 to Sebasco Estates. (Why bother to give it a number?)
2. Widest roads in the state of Maine:
   a. Maine Street in Brunswick. At 101 feet, it is almost as wide as Route 217 is long. With the traffic so heavy in the busy downtown area of Brunswick, it also provides exciting adventures should one decide to try crossing the street. Maine Street in Brunswick is so wide that when there is a parade, some schools can line their entire marching bands up in one row across.
   b. Route 1, Mars Hill. Downtown Mars Hill, with its 82-foot-wide Main Street, resembles a western cow town. Cars can easily park at an angle to the curb, and there is plenty of space for four lanes of cars (if there are that many in town at one time). Perhaps the street is so wide because it marks the confluence of two big roads—Route 1, going west toward Presque Isle, and Route 1A, going north toward Fort Fairfield. The town's wide street is made famous in the book *Women Who Come from Mars Hill and the Men Who Eat Venison.*
   c. Commercial Street, Portland. There is so much traffic—foot, auto, and formerly rail—that one forgets how wide it is (82 feet). This street was built on filled land over the edge of Portland Harbor and designed for ship commerce. Now the commerce comes not only from fishing and trade but also from tourist ships and big buses. Quaint cobble and paving stones make this an attractive feature of the Old Port area, which, in turn, places Commercial Street at the center of the battle-

ground for the future of Portland's waterfront—a battle between those who want to keep their lobster traps and those who want to create a tourist trap.

3. Places where you can go south on a northbound road: We think that the interstate system was designed to get us there faster, and the quickest way to get there from here is by means of a straight line. We would assume, therefore, that if we were headed north on Interstate 95, we would always be heading generally in a northerly direction. It's not always so. If you have a compass in your vehicle, take a look at the reading the next time you're heading from Newport to Bangor—yup, it's southerly, or southwesterly. Look at it on the map. It comes awful close to doing the same thing just outside Houlton, and it clearly does take a southerly dip as it approaches the border crossing. Of course, who could blame you for wanting to take a southerly dip in Houlton?
4. Northernmost numbered highway point: Entrance on Route 1 to the bridge between Madawaska and Edmunston, New Brunswick. Route 1 is all downhill—both east and west—from there. This bridge is famous for the thousands of people who come to Maine from Canada to buy lower-priced cigarettes, and the hundreds of Mainers who go to Canada to buy lower-priced prescription drugs.
5. Highest elevation on the state highway system: Height of Land on Route 17, in Township D, on the back road between Rumford and Rangeley. Route 17 is a beautiful road, although it is bumpy and potholed in places in summer and completely impassable at times in winter. You are likely to see a moose in one of the lower-level ponds. At its highest point, the Appalachian Trail crosses the road. When you look out over the surrounding hills and valleys, you won't think you are in Maine, but rather in the mountainous terrain of the western United States. One other thing: To many Mainers, this is the "heighth of land."

The Man Who Made Lincoln Laugh

Waterford

Christmas Eve 1863 was certainly a night to remember for twenty-eight-year-old Samuel Clemens. The young printer's apprentice and aspiring writer (he'd recently published a few articles for the local newspaper under his freshly minted pen name, Mark Twain) had spent the previous evening sitting in the front row at Maguire's Opera House in Virginia City, Nevada. According to a contemporary account, the youthful Clemens watched in utter amazement, with his jaw "literally wide open throughout the entire show," as the most famous humorist in America, Artemus Ward (the stage name of Waterford, Maine, native Charles Farrar Browne), held the standing-room-only crowd spellbound with his amazing wit, dry delivery, and pithy social commentary.

Browne was only twenty-nine years old himself when he met and mentored Mark Twain. Yet, as "Artemus Ward—The Old Showman," a character he had originally created in books and newspaper articles and later brought to life on the stage, Browne was arguably the most popular American entertainer of his day. Among his most ardent admirers was president Abraham Lincoln. Lincoln, a legendary storyteller himself and a great collector and appreciator of humor, clearly considered Artemus Ward the man to turn to when laughter was in desperately short supply.

Just five days after the bloody battle of Antietam Creek, President Lincoln called his cabinet together. There was obviously much serious and somber business to attend to. But the first thing Lincoln did was read some humorous passages from a copy of *Artemus Ward—His Book*. The reading apparently had the desired effect. There was much laughter, and the mood had lightened considerably by the time the president finished. Secretary of war Edwin M. Stanton was the only holdout. He made it clear to the president that he disapproved of such

A Maine humorist for the ages.

levity and considered it inappropriate in light of the somber circumstances of the cabinet meeting. Acknowledging the secretary's point, the president nevertheless remarked to all present, "If I did not laugh I should die, and you need this medicine as much as I do." Then he moved on to the serious business at hand. Picking up a paper from his desktop, he proceeded to read to them, for the first time, the most recent of his own writings, a document we know today as the Emancipation Proclamation.

But on that Christmas Eve in Virginia City, a young Mark Twain was wined and dined by "The Old Showman." As the evening wore on and the drinks kept coming, Twain prevailed upon his new friend to perhaps use a little of his influence to help him get a few stories published in the "big city" papers. Artemus Ward had plenty of connections. He'd been an editor and frequent contributor to *Vanity Fair,* and he promised to do what he could. He didn't forget his promise. Upon his return to Manhattan, he wrote letters on Twain's behalf, and it is very likely that Ward's advocacy led to the publication of "The Celebrated Jumping Frog of Calaveras County." The rest, where Mark Twain is concerned, is, of course, history.

The fame and fortune of Artemus Ward grew with each passing year. Constantly in demand, he packed major performing-arts venues from New York to San Francisco. In an age before mass media or electronic amplification, he performed for hundreds of thousands of adoring fans. He slept little, drank much, ate sporadically, and traveled by stagecoach and train almost constantly. At the age of thirty, he was among the wealthiest and most celebrated men in America. After a much-needed rest at his home in Waterford, Ward set sail for England in June 1866. He hit England like a comic hurricane. Huge throngs attended his comic "lectures," and he was the darling of the press. But the physical and mental strain was too much to bear. Artemus Ward, the toast of London, became too exhausted and ill to perform. He died of tuberculosis in London on March 6, 1867, at the age of thirty-three. His body was returned to America and interred at Elm Vale Cemetery in Waterford.

Today, few people visit the gravesite of this remarkable American who brought laughter to a young nation, inspired Abraham Lincoln, and helped launch the career of Mark Twain. If you do make the trip, you'll find on his tombstone the inscription "His memory will live as a sweet and unfading recollection."

Groan & McGurn's Tourist Trap

West Bethel

When visitors "from away" poke their heads into the store called Groan & McGurn's Tourist Trap, in West Bethel, they often say, "We just had to see what a tourist trap really looks like." They might be greeted with the response, "They're really not too hard to find; there's about a million of them on the highways of Maine."

The Tourist Trap started out in 1966 as the L&F Country Store. Eric Paul, whose parents owned the store, started selling T-shirts there in the late 1970s. Eric also traded T-shirts at craft shows for the goods made by potters and other craftspeople. He then sold the bartered craft items in the store. When the country store closed, the Tourist Trap opened up. Groan and McGurn were two of Eric's cats, and their names grace the establishment.

Initially, Eric said, the store sold "a lot of high-end stuff. My T-shirts were the trashiest items." Gradually, the focus of store items was on stuffed animals and refrigerator magnets—stuff the tourists like to get trapped into buying. Now, there's a lot of good stuff, mostly new, but some used, some treasures, some kitsch. As Eric says, "It's entertaining to look at and wonderful to own."

Among the maps, coffee cups, bells, and spoons that one would expect to find in a tourist trap, the store has a plastic cigar store Indian and plastic Laurel and Hardy lifesize figures. The figures look so real, Eric says, that one time a state trooper was prepared to shoot at them, thinking they were intruders. When he gets too much stuff in the store, Eric has an auction to clean out the old and to make room for the new.

The busiest time of year for the Tourist Trap is summer, as it is on the coast, although the "leaf peepers" have extended the season. People come in for directions to Canada or to Old Orchard Beach, both locations a far piece from Bethel. Eric doesn't mind giving directions, even accurate ones, because his favorite pastime is shooting the breeze with the folks he has trapped. Some people may drive by the sign, thinking it is the worst form of advertising there could be. (One road traveler put a picture of the sign on his Web blog and wrote: "Couldn't pass up a picture of the sign. We didn't stop at the store. We just took the picture and continued on down the road. In this case, it didn't pay to advertise.") But many more folks come to a screeching halt on Route 2 and step inside for the experience of truth in advertising.

The Giant Walking Serviceman

Westbrook

In the days when big people ruled the earth, there was only one person who could fix their big TVs and stereos—the Giant Walking Serviceman. Standing at the corner of Route 302 and Duck Pond Road in Westbrook, this cultural icon has been a Maine landmark for more than forty years.

The serviceman was built by Al Hawkes, who, with his father, owned a TV and radio sales and repair shop. Al was inspired by the big neon and fluorescent moving signs of the late 1940s. For example, he said, "There was a laundry in Portland that had a scrubwoman on a sign; her arms were always moving." After hiring a local artist to design the man, Al took a course in welding and hired Morin's wrecking company to put the pipes in the ground. Then he commenced to weld. It took him, his father (who was a high school teacher), and a high school kid more than six months' worth of nights and weekends to weld and assemble the statue. Al set 385 lightbulbs and additional fluorescent lighting in a circular pattern on the sign. He got a mechanical motor to move the arm back and forth as it hefted a box of TV tubes and equipment. And he put a lot of fuses in the machinery: "That way, if something went out, I could pinpoint the problem instead of taking the whole thing apart."

When he flipped the switch, sometime in 1962, it started up perfectly. The lights gleamed, the arm moved, and the man started a constant motion. In fact, people thought he was walking. But he wasn't.

"We had a contest one time, and we asked, 'How many miles has that serviceman walked over the course of its existence?' The answer was—it hasn't walked an inch." People were furious, and they insisted that it was walking. They were wrong. The only moving part was the arm; the rest, including the walking, was an illusion.

In his heyday, the Giant Walking Salesman was lit up until about 10:00 or 11:00 each evening, with light sensors getting him started and timers making sure he had a rest. The electric bill for running the guy started adding up to close to two hundred bucks a month. He became too high-maintenance for the business.

Back in 2001 Al Hawkes told me, "The day I take this guy down, I'll have an instant death. . . . A lot of people have told me this is the only point of direction they can give to get to their place, and without it, we'd all be lost." Even the bizarre comic strip *Zippy the Pinhead* has displayed the serviceman in the background.

In the summer of 2005, Al sold the building and the serviceman to a Realtor, who promptly turned it on for the first time in several years. It worked like a charm, but the local newspaper reported that the state Department of Transportation might try to shut it down as a distraction. The new owner told the paper that he might have trouble finding the switch to turn the darn thing off. So, at least for now, it's walking (or swinging) again.

Does he make house calls? I hope not!

The Big Stack—Symbol of Another Day

Westbrook

The view from the Western Promenade in Portland is spectacular. You can see mountains to the west, towns and highways spread out, and in the middle of it all, a giant smokestack. The stack, white with a black top, is the central focus of the Sappi Fine Paper factory, though long-time Mainers will recognize it as the S. D. Warren factory stack. It's unique for several reasons.

Terri Winter Messer, editor of *Sappi-Westbrook's Maine Stream,* says that at the time of its construction in 1926, it was the tallest smokestack in New England. It stands 353 feet above ground and has a diameter of 30 feet 8 inches at its base and 19 feet at the top. It took 1,990 tons of brick and 1,200 barrels of cement to construct.

Thank you for not smoking.

When it was first built, the S. D. Warren Company made fine coated magazine paper in its mill complex on the Presumpscot River. The existing smokestacks showered cinders and soda ash on the community. After the giant smokestack was built, one can assume, all of the neighboring communities got the cinders and soda ash.

The original black lettering on the stack read WARREN STANDARD PAPERS. Each letter was 6 feet high. When the Sappi company took over the Warren mill from Scott Paper in 1994, a new name was necessary. In 2000 the stack was repainted with blue letters, SAPPI FINE PAPERS. A company that specializes in painting and repairing smokestacks took five weeks to complete the job.

Each letter is 6 feet high and 12 inches thick. You might not be able to make them out from the Western Promenade, but you certainly can make them out from the Windham–Westbrook border (if you squint).

When the giant stack was built, the mill was burning coal. The cinders and the smoke were pretty toxic. Now, the plant burns wood chips, demolition wood, and debris for cogeneration, burning a lot cleaner than coal, but not without environmental concerns.

Another thing that's different from 1926 is the smell emanating from the factory. Back then, and up until the 1980s, the familiar rotten-egg odor of a kraft pulp mill wafted around town, and into Portland on westerly breezes. Nowadays, the plant doesn't produce the smell. Unfortunately, it also doesn't produce the volume of paper that Warren did. The pulp mill closed down in 1999, laying off hundreds of workers. But, the lack of smell made Westbrook a more desirable place to live. Residential values went up, even as the plant's fortunes declined.

The biggest change over time is in the symbolic nature of the giant stack. When the stack first dominated the skyline in 1926, and up until the 1990s, S. D. Warren (and Scott Paper, its successor) was by far the biggest employer, the biggest taxpayer, and the biggest benefactor in Westbrook. In 1990 there were 2,300 employees, all making good money. Now, there are 330 mill employees, working on the one remaining paper machine, and another 300 research-oriented employees in the area. Part of the reason for the decline, besides outdated mill equipment, was what was going into the atmosphere from the smokestacks of Westbrook.

If you go back to the Western Promenade in Portland and look out toward Westbrook and the giant stack, you will notice something else—the smoke in the sky isn't coming out of the big stack, as it appears to in Westbrook when you're in its shadow. It's coming out of a skinnier, taller, unpainted smokestack that is right next to it. Maybe the mill didn't want to get the giant stack's nice new paint job dirty.

Joe Perham, Maine Storyteller

West Paris

A lot of schoolteachers are comedian wannabes, dreaming of the day when they can ditch the routine of the classroom and take their routine on the road. Fortunately for audiences around the country, former Maine English teacher Joe Perham has done just that. Joe retired a few years back and took up entertaining full-time. I say fortunately because Joe is a seriously funny guy with a professionally honed native wit, which inevitably leaves his audiences weak from laughter.

Joe has cranked out no fewer than fifteen storytelling tapes of Maine humor, has appeared in films including *Graveyard Shift* and *Bed and Breakfast,* and has recorded numerous radio and TV spots. He has also appeared onstage in the persona of legendary nineteenth-century Maine humorist Artemus Ward (the pen name of humorist Charles Farrar Browne of Waterford, Maine). Browne, speaking in his A. Ward character, was a favorite of both Abe Lincoln and Mark Twain. Perham has also appeared as Holman Day, famous turn-of-the-twentieth-century Maine poet, author, and early filmmaker.

Joe Perham, Master Maine Storyteller.

Joe Perham hails from West Paris, just down the road from the Trap Corner Store, which features prominently in his monologues. He has found his niche in the pantheon of great Maine storytellers by specializing in stories about hunting and fishing. In addition to his amusing tales from the Maine woods, Joe is a virtual encyclopedia of classic New England privy, or outhouse, jokes.

His seemingly endless supply of funny lines is delivered in a natural Down East accent. But he's anything but laconic. His snappy, rapid-fire style barely lets you recover from the last line before you have to laugh at the next. You never know exactly where Joe is headed, and that's a big part of the fun. Here's an example of one of my favorite Joe Perham lines:

> *"I come from a family of fourteen kids. . . . I never slept alone 'til I was married!"*

See what I mean? Joe has graciously agreed to supply the following Top Ten Maine Outhouse Jokes. In no particular order, they are as follows:

1. A Texas senator was invited to visit some Maine businesses. Speaking from atop a farmer's manure spreader, he announced, "This is the first time I've ever been asked to speak from the Republican platform." Touring a clothespin mill, he was heard to say, "Work done on too small a scale. You got to think big to compete." The mill owner takes him to view the inventory building. "Take a look, Senator," he says. "This building has eight doors. That big enough for ya?" "Heck," says the senator, "We got outhouses in Texas bigger than this!" The mill owner replies dryly, "I guess you prob'ly need 'em, too!"

2. A father gets home late, goes upstairs to say good night to his son, and finds him kneeling behind the bed. To set a good example, he gets down on his knees and starts to pray, too. The boy says, "What are you doing, Dad?" The father replies, "Same thing you are, son." The boy says, "Mom is going to be awfully mad. There's only one pot in here!"

3. On a Maine farm, after fall cleaning, Grammie pours liquid naphtha down the privy hole. Grampa goes out there, sits a spell, lights his pipe, and drops a burning match down the hole. An explosion

results. Grampa says (pick one): A. "I'm glad I didn't try to sneak that one out in the kitchen!" B. "It must'a been somethin' I 'et!" After this incident, Grampa installs brass handles on the seat to help hold himself down if it ever happens again.

4. This heavy fella goes into an outhouse at a Maine fairground late one evening. As he sits down, the seat gives way, dropping him 7 feet below. He starts hollering, "Fire! Fire!" A crew of firemen arrives shortly and hauls him out. The fire chief asks, "How come you hollered 'Fire!'?" To which the heavyset man replies, "How many people you think would'a showed up if I'd hollered what I was really into?"

5. The morning after Halloween, a father asks his son if he knows who pushed over the family privy the night before, reminding the boy how George Washington confessed to cutting down the cherry tree. The boy admits that he and his friend were the culprits, and his dad proceeds to "whale the tar" out of him. The kid cries, "When George Washington told the truth, he didn't get a lickin'. How come I did?" His dad says, "When George Washington cut down the cherry tree, his father wasn't sitting in it. That's how come!"

6. A woman from rural Maine, having lived her life serviced by an old-fashioned privy, finally moves into a new home equipped with a "water closet," an early commode popular in New England. She writes to her son, "Our new home has a washing machine, but it don't work too good. I put in fourteen shirts, pulled the chain, ain't seen the shirts since! It had two lids on it; I used one for a breadboard. The other one had a hole in it, so I used it to frame Grampa's pitcha."

7. A man put a fresh coat of varnish on the toilet seat in his outhouse, but he forgot to put a sign on the door. His wife went in, locked the

door, and settled in. When she tried to get up, she couldn't. Her husband had to break down the door, unhook the seat, and carry her into the doctor's office with the seat still attached. The nurse said, "Ever seen a sight like that, Doc?" He replied, "Yes, but this is the first time I've ever seen one framed!"

8. Fred and Ed were out hunting. Fred went behind a bush to seek some relief and sat right down on a bear trap that was chained to the bush. At the hunting camp later, Ed said, "The sound that came out of Fred was the second loudest noise I ever heard in my life." Someone asked, "The second loudest?" Ed says, "Yeah, the first loudest noise I ever heard was when Fred hit the end of that chain!"

9. Maine selectmen traditionally have had buildings equipped with a two-hole outhouse. Occasionally town folk have suggested that it would be more appropriate if they had a one holer so that the selectmen wouldn't be forced to make a decision. Some even suggested a one-half holer—for what reason we can only surmise.

10. Selectmen's duties often involve inspecting privies. There's a tale of one selectman who informed a woman that she'd have to move her privy because it was "too close to running water." She says, "Who are you to tell me what to do?" He says, "I'm the privy inspector." She says, "Good. I'm having trouble with my privy." He says, "What's the problem?" She says, "You're the privy inspector. You tell me." So he checks the structure, outside and in, going so far as to stick his head down inside the hole. As he pulls his head out, his beard gets caught in a crack in the seat. He hollers, "Ouch, my beard's caught! I'm stuck!" To which she responds, "Irritatin', ain't it?"

Painting the Barter Family Tree

West Sullivan

In a state known for its artists, Philip Barter is a real breath of fresh air. His paintings, sculptures, carvings, and wildly original furniture seem almost alive. Full of brilliant colors and playful forms, Phil's creations are bursting at the seams with the pure joy of the visual experience. Philip Barter is a native Mainer, one of the Boothbay Barters (from Barter's Island, no less) and darn proud of it. He laughingly says that there are rumors around to the effect that his forebears—the original Barter's Island Barters—may have actually rowed here from England back in the late sixteenth or early seventeenth century. I don't know about that. But if those early Barters had half the energy Phil does, it's certainly possible.

These days you can find Phil, his wife, Priscilla, and a random selection of other Barter family members at the Barter Family Gallery in West Sullivan. The gallery was Phil's idea. After enduring the requisite "starving artist" period, which painters with Phil's talent always seem destined to endure, his work finally started to take off big time back in the late 1980s. A major retrospective of his paintings at Bates College in 1992 solidified his growing reputation as one of the great contemporary Maine painters.

Now, all that acclaim and recognition must have felt good. But keep in mind that Phil came up the hard way. As a Barter from Barter's Island, he certainly appreciated the substantial fees his work was finally bringing in, but chafed at the 50 percent commissions the galleries sliced off the top. That's how he tells it, anyway. Frankly, I think the true motivation behind the Barter Family Gallery is more personal. I just think Phil would rather hang around painting, mentoring, and encouraging his brood of incredibly talented kids than stand around sipping flat Chablis at a stuffy gallery opening.

Whatever the Barters' motivation for starting their enterprise, the gallery itself is not to be missed. It's pretty easy to find, too. Just take Route 1 North out of Ellsworth; after you cross the Hancock/Sullivan Bridge, keep your eyes peeled for a sign that reads BARTER FAMILY GALLERY 2½ MILES. Hang a left, follow the signs along the way, and literally, you can't miss it. The gallery, on the right-hand side of the road, looks more or less like the aftermath of an explosion at a paint factory. Over the years, the Barters have carefully hand-painted nearly every visible surface of the whole rambling structure. Mullions, sills, archways, etc., shimmer in a variety of arresting colors. There are paintings everywhere, inside and out, brilliantly hued sculptures all around the grounds, and wildly painted furniture set about the yard. The whole place has a fanciful fairy-tale quality that just cries out for exploration.

Mostly, Phil and Priscilla are around (if not, just jot a note on the pad by the side of the door), and chatting with them is a huge part of the fun. Although Phil has had major surgery (completely successful, he assures me), he has lost none of his zest for life. Whether you end up buying something or not, just poking around the place will give you enough visual stimulation to last you for several weeks.

That would be Phil on the left . . . and Phil on the right.

I know you'll have a good time with the Barter family. But I must warn you, their creativity is infectious, and side effects may develop. After you've been through the gallery and made your way back home, you're apt to find that the old pine chairs in your living room are suddenly starting to look a little dowdy. That's usually the first symptom. If you catch yourself lingering over paintbrushes and little cans of bright purple, fire engine red, and lemon yellow high-gloss enamel, you can be pretty sure that you've caught the "Barter bug." If you're as lucky as Phil, you'll find that it's incurable.

Babb's Bridge

Windham

When I was a lad, my friends and I went to Babb's Bridge, a covered bridge that spans the Presumpscot River between Windham and Gorham. We jumped off its lower trusses into the Presumpscot. Some brave souls jumped from the roof of the bridge, others jumped in by means of the tire swing on the tree next to it. Cars and trucks would beep their horns as they entered the bridge, then you would hear their tires thunk on the wooden floor and make the same crossing that horse-drawn wagons did more than 150 years ago when the bridge was built. This was as bucolic as you could get, and it was the same river that, as it went downstream, powered mighty paper mills and became a foul sewer as it flowed into the sea.

The opportunities for swimming might be gone today, but there's still a covered bridge. By car, or horse, just go north on River Road toward North Windham. About 1½ miles after the intersection with Route 202, turn left at the sign and go about another ½ mile to Babb's Bridge.

There you'll find Babb's Bridge, a replica of the original, which had been built in 1864 using the Howe truss method of construction. (This was either a method of construction or something the workers who carried the heavy beams had to wear.) Upon entering the structure (beep first to alert oncoming traffic) your wheels touch the wooden floor, which is suspended on a series of "chords," or heavy beams, set parallel to the roadway. You will notice the post-and-beam construction of the timbers supporting the roof. It's cozy in there, like being in an old barn.

There are only eight covered bridges left in Maine, according to the state's Department of Transportation. There once were 120, but they have been washed away or rotted out. Babb's Bridge and the other covered bridges were constructed to keep the rain and snow off the timbers holding up the structure and, in many cases, forming the roadway. This reduced the rot and swelling. The remaining bridges have survived for 150 years, so their coverings actually served their noble purpose.

In 1985 the Maine legislature authorized the Department of Transportation to maintain and preserve covered bridges that weren't part of the state highway system. Babb's Bridge was doing well keeping out natural elements, but it couldn't withstand the onslaught of humans. In 1973 vandals burned the structure. An "exact replica" was constructed on the site and opened in 1976.

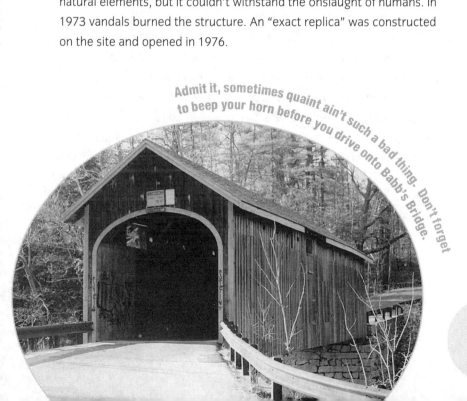

Admit it, sometimes quaint ain't such a bad thing. Don't forget to beep your horn before you drive onto Babb's Bridge.

Those less bucolically inclined might wonder why our tax dollars have gone to reconstruct a covered bridge, when a steel and metal and asphalt structure would cost less and be more reliable. Perhaps a cost-benefit analysis was performed, showing that tourists will shell out more money when they have these quaint amenities. Or perhaps it was because we like the old covered bridges and we want to keep a few of 'em around. At any rate, Babb's Bridge should be there for another 150 years, if the vandals keep away and the river doesn't rise too much.

Maine's Biggest Small Eatery

Wiscasset

There's no surer sign that tourist season has hit the Maine coast than a swarm of tourists and locals around Red's Eats on an early summer evening. You never know who you're going to run into at Red's. A few summers back Tom Cruise hopped out of a stretch limo to pick up some hot dogs and an order of fries to go.

Red's Eats, situated on the western end of the Wiscasset bridge since 1938, is a classic example of the New England Clam Shack school of architecture, and the basic menu is pretty much what you'd expect. Besides burgers and dogs, you've got your french fries, fried onion rings, fried shrimp, fried haddock, fried clams, fried scallops . . . are you beginning to notice a trend here? I haven't checked with the American Heart Association or anything, but it's a safe bet that an average meal at Red's will take care of your maximum daily recommended cholesterol intake for pretty much the rest of the summer.

And they're not resting on their laurels, either. The motto at Red's Eats might as well be "When better artery busters are built, we'll build 'em!" Of course, you can't go wrong with the world-famous-since-1938 "sturdly," a grilled hot dog split down the middle and stuffed with

American cheese. But if you don't happen to own a bathroom scale and you're feeling lucky today, why not plunge right into Red's latest creation, the aptly named "puff dog," a split wiener, liberally stuffed with bacon and cheese, then rolled in heavy batter and, you guessed it, deep fried.

Are you tired of paying an arm and a leg for a lobster roll with a couple of ounces of lobster and a quarter pound of iceberg lettuce? You came to the right place. Although you may want to check with your broker before treating the family to lobster rolls at Red's, at least nobody will be complaining about the serving size. A few years back, Red (that's owner Al Gagnon, who has been slaving over a hot fry-o-lator at Red's for more than a quarter century) started making his lobster rolls with "at *least*," he says, "a whole pound of lobster meat in each one!" And the price? "Market price," says Al. That's currently somewhere between twelve and fourteen bucks a pop. Maybe a few "sturdlies" would be a more responsible choice, after all. Either way, you'll have fun. Just don't mention this little outing to your cardiologist, OK?

Folks drop by Red's for fried everything and celebrity gawking.

THE YORKS AND THE BERWICKS

One of the first things people used to see when entering the state of Maine from New Hampshire on I–95 was a big green sign, resembling the other green signs on the turnpike, which directed people to the next exit in order to see "The Yorks and The Berwicks."

Over the years, many questions have been raised about this sign. Basically, the questions boil down to one: Who the heck are the Yorks and the Berwicks? Here are some, chosen at random, from index cards left at the tollbooth.

- Maine is, after all, the home of giants—the Walking Serviceman, Sardine Man, the Big Indians, and others. Was there an entire race of people so big that they earned their own sign on the turnpike?
- Was Maine so small that every family had its own sign?
- Do you have to pay extra to have your family name on the sign?
- Weren't these the two feuding families in one of those Shakespearean plays? Did they ever intermarry? Would a youthful York be shot if he was seen making eyes at a bashful Berwick?
- There has been some speculation that if one, in fact, took the exit, one might soon end up in the town of York. Was this a town named after the people who are on this sign?

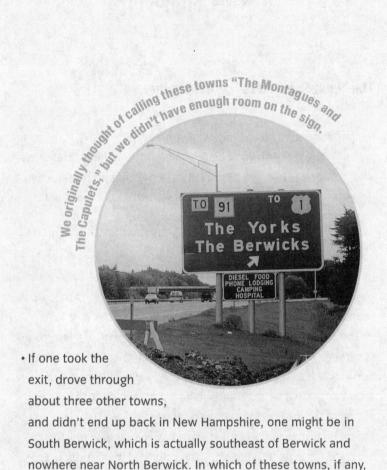

We originally thought of calling these towns "The Montagues and The Capulets," but we didn't have enough room on the sign.

- If one took the exit, drove through about three other towns, and didn't end up back in New Hampshire, one might be in South Berwick, which is actually southeast of Berwick and nowhere near North Berwick. In which of these towns, if any, do "the Berwicks" live?

Times have changed, though, and the Yorks and the Berwicks are no longer on the same sign. In fact, the Berwicks are pretty much ignored these days. The towns are exactly where they were before, so it must be that the families either moved or felt the need for some anonymity. Perhaps they concluded, "Everyone sees our sign and thinks they can just drop in."

The "Lost Schooners" of Wiscasset

Wiscasset

Hesper and Luther will be missed. For many folks, the little riverside village of Wiscasset just won't be the same without the familiar old salts sitting side by side down by the banks of the Sheepscott. Where did they go? Well, in a sense, like Douglas MacArthur's famous old soldiers, they just "faded away"—and thereby hangs a tale.

The names I just mentioned are not those of venerable senior citizens (although, in some sense, perhaps they might as well be). Nope, Hesper and Luther are (or were) a pair of aging coastal schooners, *The Hesper* and *The Luther Little,* which for the better part of a century sat abandoned in the mudflats at the western end of the Wiscasset bridge.

The hard truth is that the age of sail, that halcyon era when proud, square-rigged schooners crowded the shipping lanes, lines taut, sails billowing, hauling Maine timber, ice, and sardines to distant ports, ended not with a whimper but with a bang—the bang of a steam engine. Almost overnight these graceful wooden-hulled "ladies of the sea" were just plain obsolete, eclipsed by steam-powered vessels, capable of making deliveries on time with or without a stiff breeze.

Up and down the Maine coast, hundreds of these once proud vessels were unceremoniously (and illegally) dumped in the nearest harbor or along a riverbank. For many they were just a nuisance and a hazard to navigation. But they were too big to haul off, and where would you put them, anyway? Who would pay for the job? So these ships just sat rotting away in the mud, looking about as romantic to the locals as a pair of abandoned Chevys rusting on the front lawn.

Fortunately, the tourists saw them in a different light. Painters and photographers started coming around to capture their salty essence, Charles Kuralt featured them in one of his famous "On the Road" stories for CBS News, and before you knew it, a major tourist attraction had been born. The image of the abandoned schooners soon became pretty much the official symbol of Wiscasset.

A restaurant called Le Garage opened on the riverbank, and its menu featured a sketch of Hester and Luther. It was always a big deal to get there early enough to claim a choice table overlooking the hulking barnacle-clad derelicts. Postcards and note cards and T-shirts emblazoned with the image of the schooners flooded the town. Even the town seal, reproduced on official stationery and emblazoned on the doors of local police cruisers, features Wiscasset's famous senior citizens.

Naturally, you want to go take a look at them, right? Sorry 'bout that! You see, while folks were busy cranking out postcards and T-shirts and menus and knickknacks of the schooners, the actual ships themselves were doing the only thing they could do under the circumstances. They were rotting away.

Mercifully, the end came quickly. Following a particularly blustery midnight storm back in the mid-1990s, early-morning commuters, lobstermen heading out to tend their traps, and everybody else who glanced in their direction got a rude shock. The schooners, which had sat there for almost a century, were gone. Just gone.

Don't take it too hard, though. Wiscasset still bears the ghostly imprint of these famous wrecks, and as long as there are tourist dollars to be snagged, you'll still be able to buy a nice set of note cards with a sketch of *The Hester* and *The Luther Little* on them. There is also one other plus: As you travel around Maine, you'll notice that the natives have an irritating habit of giving directions based on landmarks that no longer exist. So don't be surprised if, when asking a local for directions to Fort Edgecomb, he says, "Drive down to Wiscasset, then cross the bridge right where them old ships used to be . . ." Call me romantic, but I say there's something kinda comforting in knowing that Mainers will still be using these old salts as a landmark a century or two after they gave up the ghost.

FOLLOW YOUR "DREMS"

For some reason, the dozen or so miles of coastal Route 1 from the east bank of the Kennebec River in Woolwich to the west bank of the Sheepscott in Wiscasset has, over the years, become a magnet for roadside vendors. It's anybody's guess how this happened, but I think it probably has something to do with traffic congestion. Traditionally, both the Bath bridge and the one in Wiscasset have been notorious summertime bottlenecks. Despite the DOT's best efforts to move things along (both bridges have been widened in recent years), you might just as well accept the fact that you'll be doing a lot of idling, downshifting, and gawking on this particular stretch between July 4 and Labor Day.

That's OK. This is Maine, remember? Life in the slow lane? Depending on the time of year, you're going to have plenty of opportunities to stop and purchase a dizzying array of products, from fresh farm produce to homemade handcrafts to discounted designer jeans as you crawl inexorably toward your final destination. Take the right attitude, and this ribbon of bumper to bumper, two-lane Maine blacktop might just be the ultimate cure for road rage. You might as well relax. Ain't NOBODY goin' anywhere fast on this road today.

Meanwhile, as you ponder the fluid level in your radiator and whether or not you remembered to ask for guaranteed late arrival at your motel, you'll notice that there are an inordinate number of ancient Dodge Aspen station wagons and old pickup trucks lining the soft shoulder. Parked on folding chairs under faded beach umbrellas, a variety of 3Ms (Mainers of Modest Means) peddle their wares. What wares? Well, bunches of sea grass (a lovely lavender

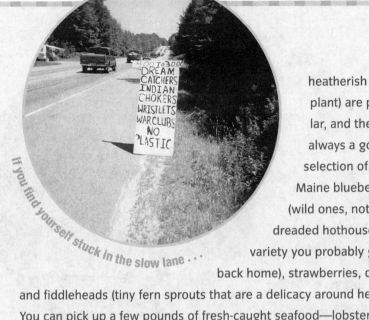

If you find yourself stuck in the slow lane . . .

heatherish plant) are popular, and there's always a good selection of fresh Maine blueberries (wild ones, not the dreaded hothouse variety you probably get back home), strawberries, corn, and fiddleheads (tiny fern sprouts that are a delicacy around here). You can pick up a few pounds of fresh-caught seafood—lobster, clams, mussels, crabs, haddock, etc.—direct from the fisherman, at reasonable prices. Sometimes there are handcrafted items like whirligigs and homemade lawn art. The variety is endless. In fact, if there's such a thing as an oil-on-velvet painting of a lighthouse being produced in Maine, you're likely to see it here first.

Oh yeah, a big part of the fun is reading the homemade plywood signs propped up on the soft shoulder. One of my favorites, a particularly enthusiastic, "rustic" hand-lettered job on an oddly shaped rectangle of warped plywood, promises DREM

. . . why not stop . . .

CONTINUED

. . . and pick up a bargain or two!

CATCHERS! $3 EACH! 500 FEET AHEAD!! Drem catchers? It took a second to translate that. I realized as I drove by that the sign was referring to dream catchers, handmade Native American folk art. That seemed particularly fitting for this bit of highway, where the unspoken message seems to be "You too can have a tourist business in Maine." Apparently all it takes is an old station wagon, a hand-painted plywood sign, and a "drem."

The stretch of road between Woolwich and Wiscasset is not just noted for bottlenecks. It also has a high number of traffic accidents. The August 13, 2005, *Portland Press Herald* reported that, in an effort to "shrink" the number of accidents, the state DOT hired a psychologist to work with engineers in redesigning the road, taking into account drivers' behavior when faced with the type of road conditions that might lead to accidents. Perhaps the psychologist should be asked, "What do my drems mean?"

A Matter of "Taste"

Woolwich

When Larry Crooker, owner of the Taste of Maine restaurant in Woolwich, first clapped his eyeballs on the giant bucktoothed lobster welded together from rusty abandoned oil drums, he wasn't particularly pleased at the sight. The odd, oxidizing crustacean simply appeared out of nowhere one Monday morning parked on an abandoned broken-down trailer right in the middle of his restaurant parking lot in Woolwich, right in the middle of tourist season. He had no idea how it got there, who it belonged to, or how to remove it. It just sat there being an eyesore and taking up precious tourist parking spots. According to Larry, "It was kinda in the way, and we were wonderin' what it was gonna take to get it outta there."

Over the next few days, however, Larry's attitude began to change. "The people [hungry tourists] kept lookin' at this thing, and we kept lookin' at it, and it kinda grew on us," he says. "After a few days, when he finally came around ["he" being the sculptor Robert Daniels of St. George, Maine, who was towing his creation to an art exhibit in Kittery

I never claimed that Maine lobsters are always in good taste. I just said that they always taste good.

when a broken trailer axle forced him to abandon it in the restaurant's parking lot], we decided it was kind of an attraction."

The enthusiastic reaction of his customers had expanded Larry's artistic sensibilities considerably. Acting on his newfound "taste" for monumental sculpture, Larry purchased the lobster for $2,500 on the spot. His own creative spirit now liberated, he set to work "sprucing it up" for its new role as a famous Maine culinary landmark. "My father had some of these big metal buoys they have in the ocean." (Surprised? Don't be. Nobody ever throws anything away in Maine. You never know when it'll come in handy.) "We put them around it. Then we put some lobster traps around it." (Piling old wooden lobster traps on just about anything, from a rusted-out Buick to a granite boulder, is a time-honored marketing technique along Maine's coastal Route 1.) "We had a little sign made that says THE TASTE OF MAINE on it. Because the people kept gettin' around it takin' pictures of it, we wanted everybody to know where it is." (Natch.) "And then we painted it bright red" (always a good idea with a giant lobster in these parts) "so when you come up over the hill there, it kinda hits you right in the eye."

That it does. And when you're trolling for tourist dollars along the Maine coast, "hittin' 'em right in the eye" is what it's all about.

EARTHA

Yarmouth

Maine has the big stuff, all right: the Paul Bunyan statue, the Big Indians, the objects that appear larger-than-life-size. But what about a roadside attraction that is only one one-millionth of its size—and yet represents something that is bigger than anything on earth? Of course, it would have to be a scale model of the earth itself, affectionately known as EARTHA. It can be found spinning on its axis at the DeLorme

Right around midnight, this place starts to look like a scene from a Steven Spielberg flick.

Map Store on the Freeport-Yarmouth line, just about a mile south of the Freeport Big Indian.

Built in 1998, EARTHA is a giant globe, 43 feet in diameter. According to Andy Sturtevant, public relations manager at DeLorme, this is one one-millionth of the earth's actual diameter. How was the earth's diameter originally measured? By overpaid government workers with tape measures? Not quite. The surface of this globe was designed on the basis of satellite photography and ocean studies, as well as by using information from DeLorme's own maps. At any rate, EARTHA is so big that you can spot the state of Maine, but it does not show political boundaries (so you can't see the New Hampshire tollbooth). You might not even be able to tell how to get to East Vassalboro.

At night EARTHA lights up and appears, to people on the road, to be floating. Actually, it's spinning on its own axis, which has different time settings for rotations. Andy says the actual rotation time of one day would be too slow to be interesting, so EARTHA rotates once every seventeen minutes. Talk about time flying by! Hey, it's 2:17 P.M. and another day has gone by.

EARTHA is part of the EARTHA Educational Alliance, a project that teaches kids about maps. In an earlier time, all we knew about maps was what we learned from the fold-out ones sold at gas stations. In these new, enlightened times, maps are more accurate and complex. One thing that has remained the same, however, is that they are still impossible to fold up properly on the first try—unless you have attended the EARTHA Educational Alliance. Andy says kids really love to visit EARTHA. Some of them aren't sure what it is and say, "Hey mom, look at the big ball."

There haven't been any reports of inaccuracy of topography (say, like making Greenland bigger than South America or putting Florida next to the Georgia that really belongs next to Russia). There also haven't been any protests from the Flat Earth Society, which plans to put its own version of the world on a less-traveled road. Andy says that several visitors have speculated that EARTHA was constructed from a do-it-yourself "kitt." (Eartha Kitt, get it?) Great minds think alike.

As for the future, don't expect a Sun, a Moon, or a Mars-tha. EARTHA was the vision of David DeLorme, and, according to Andy, David has mixed feelings about the project. "He'll take the best offer for it," Andy says. Which raises the question, who would move it? Atlas Van Lines?

EARTHA is open to visitors at no charge whenever the DeLorme Map Store is open. You can visit EARTHA seven days a week from 8:30 A.M. to 8:00 P.M. in summer and during somewhat abbreviated hours in the winter. You don't have to leave Maine to see the entire world!

INDEX

INDEX

INDEX

INDEX

INDEX

About the Authors

Tim Sample was born and raised in the state of Maine. His books, albums, and videos of Down East humor, including four albums recorded for the Bert and I company, have sold more than two million copies. Tim has performed throughout America and has appeared on numerous national TV broadcasts, including *The Today Show* and *Good Morning America,* and Michael Feldman's hit radio show, *Whad'Ya Know?* From 1993 through 2004 Tim was a regular correspondent for the Emmy award–winning *CBS Sunday Morning.*

Tim lives in Brunswick, Maine, with his wife, Kevin Sample-Wilcox, and when he's not in the recording studio or on tour, they're apt to be rusticating at their cabin in Washington County, Maine, or exploring the back roads of New England on Tim's motorcycle or in their vintage Mercedes roadster "Zelda."

For more information please visit the Web site www.TimSample.com.

Steve Bither is an attorney practicing in Portland. He is a member of the Wicked Good Band, a musical comedy group that has been performing at festivals and concerts in Maine and around the country for more than twenty-five years. He is also the pianist in a jazz band that plays in convalescent homes in the Portland area. In 1985 he published *The Wicked Good Book,* a best-selling collection of Maine humor.